soul food

52 PRINCIPLES OF BLACK ENTREPRENEURIAL SUCCESS

Robert L. Wallace

PERSEUS PUBLISHING

Cambridge, Massachusetts

Perseus Publishing is a member of the Perseus Books Group

Find Perseus Publishing on the World Wide Web at
http://www.perseuspublishing.com

Perseus Publishing books are available at special discounts for bulk purchases in the U.S. by corporations, institutions, and other organizations. For more information, please contact the Special Markets Department at HarperCollins Publishers, 10 East 53rd Street, New York, NY 10022, or call 1–212–207–7528.

Library of Congress Catalog Card Number: 00-102291
ISBN: 0–7382–0352-1

Text design by Cynthia Young
Set in 10-point Stone Serif by the Perseus Books Group

1 2 3 4 5 6 7 8 9 10—03 02 01 00
First printing, August 2000

Contents

PART TWO
Principles of Building Entrepreneurial Success   71

PART THREE
Principles of Entrepreneurship Maintenance   125

PART FOUR
Principles of Self-Actualization   **209**

Acknowledgments

In my first book, *Black Wealth Through Black Entrepreneurship* (Duncan & Duncan, 1993), the acknowledgments I listed ended up requiring more than five pages to capture. I promised myself that the next time around I would not be so verbose.

In my followup book, *Black Wealth: The Road to Small Business Success* (John Wiley & Sons, 2000), I was able to reduce the acknowledgment section to three pages.

Now, in this my third book project, *Soul Food: 52 Principles of Black Entrepreneurial Success,* I will attempt to keep the trend moving in the same direction, but I know that will be difficult.

The task is more difficult because the older I become, the more I realize how important people are to me and the integral role we all play in each other's success. I have so many people to thank but so little time and space to do it in. For those I might fail to mention, please forgive me.

As is my habit, let me first give honor to God, my ancestors, and my parents for bringing me into this world and for blessing me with a rich, robust, and proud legacy that gives me stability and purpose in these uncertain times.

My sincere gratitude and love to my beautiful wife Carolyn and our five marvelous children, Robert Jr., Joshua, Collin, Jordan-David, and Taylor Irene, whose unwavering love gives me hope in a world that is becoming increasingly hopeless.

Special blessings and thanks to my outstanding book agent, Andrea Pedolsky of Altair Literary Agency, and Jacqueline Murphy, my editor at Perseus Books. These ladies have taken very good care of me, and I am grateful.

A special thanks to George Blake, a young and very talented professional who was invaluable in assisting me in researching and completing *Soul Food*. George, I pray that your dream of becoming a Hollywood television show writer and producer will become a reality very soon.

I am forever indebted to the staff of my two companies, The BiTH Group, Inc. and EntreTeach.com, L.L.C. Without my team, it would be impossible for me to do the things that matter most. A deep and sincere thank you to my special teammates Harry W. Holt Jr., Josephine Blake, and Vesta Jackson-Crute for seeing and believing in the dream.

Last, I want to thank the hundreds of black, Hispanic, Asian, Native American, and women entrepreneurs who trusted me enough to share their most intimate thoughts and experiences surrounding the principles of entrepreneurial success. Thank you for caring and for believing in this book.

This book is humbly dedicated to our Lord and Savior, Jesus Christ, who sits at the right hand of the Father and who will soon return to escort us to our majestic home, located somewhere on the outskirts of eternity. May all of God's people keep moving onward and upward!

Soul Food is also dedicated to my beautiful and loving wife Carolyn, affectionately known as "Kelly," who is a wonderful blessing from God and who in conjunction with the Father has conspired to make all of my dreams come true. Every day that I look into her caring eyes, I am reminded of just how much God truly loves me.

Introduction

The captain of a United States naval destroyer was participating in a training exercise off the Atlantic coast during a major winter storm. The billows were rising, and the sky was dark and threatening. To make matters worse, a heavy fog had settled in, making visibility almost impossible. While the captain was on the bridge, navigating his vessel through the perilous storm, the ship's lookout spotted off the left bow a faint light in the distance. He notified the captain of his sighting.

Thinking that the light might represent another vessel traveling in the sea-lane, the captain asked the lookout, " Is it steady or moving?"

"It's steady," the lookout replied.

Hearing this, the captain called to the signalman, "Signal the ship—'Advise that you adjust your navigation coordinates by 20 degrees to avoid collision.'"

A few seconds later, a signal returned from the direction of the distant light. "Cannot oblige your request. You must adjust your coordinates by 20 degrees or we will collide!"

Startled, the captain signaled again that the approaching ship adjust its coordinates lest they both perish. To his dismay, there was no reply.

By this time, the captain of the destroyer was getting angry, frustrated, and fearful. Shipwrecks were the stuff of legends to him. He had never expected to be faced with this moment. The light that was once far away in the distance had now moved closer and was frighteningly more distinct.

Nervously, the captain bellowed to the signalman one more time. "Send—'Adjust your vessel by 20 degrees. I am a captain in the United States Navy, the most powerful navy in the world!'" The captain hoped his bravado would fend off the impending disaster. All of his years as a seaman had come to this point; standing on his merit seemed a logical resolution.

After a few frantic seconds, a response came that put everything into perspective. A light flashing through the foggy mist replied, "Captain, you must adjust your course. I am the lighthouse!"

This experience shared by Frank Koch in *Proceedings*, the magazine of the Naval Institute, helps to make two key points. The first point is that like the abiding success principles introduced in this book, the lighthouse does not move. It is permanent and is not altered or changed.

The second point is that just as enduring principles are meant to guide us through life, the lighthouse is used to guide ships into safe waters and away from the treacherous, surf-battered shores. If a ship ignores the lighthouse and mistakenly moves too close to the rocks or gets caught in the powerful riptides or undercurrents of merging masses of water, it could be torn apart in a matter of minutes.

The 52 principles of black entrepreneurial success presented in this book serve the same purpose by providing entrepreneurs guidance and safe passage as they navigate their way through the tight straits of the economy and successfully dock their ships at the port of entrepreneurial success.

Unfortunately, many minority and women entrepreneurs sail into treacherous waters unknowingly. Like the naval captain, they sometimes fail to heed the intermittent warnings of the lighthouse (principles). The tragedy of this situation, though, is that they have no reason to be at such great risk. The majority of entrepreneurs are confident, highly educated, experienced, task-oriented, and moderately successful in their own right. Despite many years of experience and good technical skills, many are oblivious to the light-houses that stand ready to direct their journey toward long-term success as entrepreneurs. Providing guidance and direction, the principles in this book have stood the test of time and serve to provide much-needed light in a sea of darkness. In short, each principle is a lighthouse. After many years of research studying minority and female entre-preneurs, I am convinced that a clear understanding of these principles will dictate how these entrepreneurs can ultimately find success. Although the names and locations of the entrepreneurs have been changed, the principles demonstrated by their stories are powerful.

Knowledge of these principles is one thing, but applying them is another. Knowledge improperly applied is useless to the entrepreneur. Therefore, entrepreneurs must take responsibility and adjust their business strategies to remain in harmony with these unchanging principles. As the cap-tain of the vessel eventually realized, failure to abide by the directions of the lighthouse (principles) can eventually lead to failure. The purpose of this book is to provide guidance and understanding on the underlying business strategies that impact black entrepreneurial success in America.

Getting Past the Immediate
Isn't Always Easy

Soul Food directs the entrepreneur to move quickly beyond the important immediate or primary entrepreneurial tasks and introduces the secondary tasks of discovering and using the entrepreneurial principles of success.

These rudimentary tasks include such matters as develop-ing a business concept, building a business strategy, access-ing financing, developing effective marketing strategies, and writing business plans. Secondary tasks addressed in this book are the intangible tasks that, like the air we breathe, cannot be seen, touched, or heard but can be felt.

The impact of these secondary tasks is just as critical and discernible as that of the tactile primary tasks.

My research shows that due to the "isms"—racism, sexism, ageism, and classism—many minority and female entrepreneurs are forced to spend the majority of their resources focusing only on the immediate or primary tasks and ignoring the more elusive secondary entrepreneurial tasks. The current public debate on the appropriateness of affirmative action and the misplaced rhetoric about America's inherent meritocracy have thrown many entrepreneurs off course and forced some into panic mode. This strategy often leaves these entrepreneurs frustrated, angry, confused, and disillusioned.

How the 52 Principles Are Presented

Some might ask, why 52 principles? First, this book is a learning tool that directs the reader to review one principle weekly with the goal of internalizing each principle. Internalizing the 52 principles will require time and a commitment to restructure how you think and how you conduct your business affairs each day. It will require you to challenge your paradigms about entrepreneurship, success, racism, sexism, and the relationship that you have with members of different races and genders. To apply these principles successfully, you should perform six specific tasks each week:

1. Invest in a sturdy leather-bound journal that is easy to write in and will stand up to heavy use. Carry this journal with you at all times and treat it as something very valuable. At the beginning of the week on Sunday, write the principle for that week at the top of the page and begin documenting any thoughts that come to mind then or at anytime during that week.

2. Begin studying the specific principle on the same day you attend church service. People typically are in a spiritual and receptive mood after a religious service; the mind tends to be open to new ideas and paradigm challenges. If you don't attend regular church services, then set aside a day each week to begin some process or meditation that is self-affirming and spiritually renewing.

3. Think about and list examples of how the principle has either already been put to use in your business experiences or how it could be used as a part of your revised strategy.

4. Study the specifics of the principle and understand how it works. Each chapter provides enough details and information for you to test and apply the principles to your specific experiences.

5. Share the principle with someone else. Explain to the person your understanding of how the principle works and how you plan to apply it.

6. Apply the principle within 36 hours of being introduced to it. Over time, observe the results.

The 52 principles are organized into four strategic categories:

- Entrepreneurship preparation
- Entrepreneurship development
- Entrepreneurship maintenance
- Entrepreneurship self-actualization

The category that most benefits you will be a function of where you are on the entrepreneurship development spectrum (e.g., embryonic, emerging, established). For example, if you are an emerging entrepreneur, you will probably want to review the principles in all four categories. If you are an established entrepreneur, you may be more interested in studying the principles for self-actualization. An embryonic entrepreneur may desire to focus initially on the principles that pertain to building a business and then review the principles on maintaining the business, once it has grown to a specific point.

Soul Food introduces success principles to the reader through short, heartwarming true stories that were shared with me by successful black and minority entrepreneurs over the past twenty years. Each story has an accompanying principle to be meditated upon for the week. Whether I heard a story over a plate of freshly picked collard greens on the back porch of a southern estate, or in the cockpit of a four-seat Cessna, all of these stories were told with candor and humor overflowing with wisdom, insight, and spirituality.

Each story illustrates how an individual was introduced to the principle and how he or she was able to leverage the event to help achieve a specific business goal. In some cases, the entrepreneur may have lacked knowledge of the principle and thus been negatively impacted.

Following each anecdote is a technical analysis of the pertinent principle. This analysis breaks the principle down into smaller components that are easily understandable and applicable. To conclude the review of the principle, a list of tactical "to dos" should be documented in your journal. These "to dos" should be completed immediately to begin implementing the principle discussed.

As you read these stories, you can pretend you are positioned around a campfire being mentored by the village elders. Imagine the flames flickering in their eyes as they orally pass on the lessons, trials, and ultimate triumphs of a great and noble class of people. Listen carefully to their stories and learn!

PART ONE

Principles of Entrepreneurship Preparation

1

The Leveraging of Gratitude Principle

The Designer's Designer

Most women in the neighborhood looked up to Karen. Although many of them were either unwed mothers or substance abusers, Karen exuded a sense of hope that was important to them, and she provided a role model. In this neighborhood of rat-infested dwellings, drug-dealing corners, and nervous, trigger-happy police officers, someone like Karen was indeed a breath of fresh air.

Although it didn't show in Karen's outlook and appearance, she emerged from rough beginnings. After graduating at the top of her class from academically advanced Eastern High School, she had her choice of college scholarships. Not only were the state schools interested in her, but the Ivy Leaguers were calling as well. Harvard, Yale, and Brown were all interested in this petite, bright, little black girl with long black braids that rested on her shoulders.

College had always been a dream of Karen's, but marriage was also high on her list of priorities. Typical for her peer group, Karen fell in love with her high school sweetheart, Elroy. Elroy, though only an average student, was an outstanding athlete who excelled in football and basketball. Elroy's charm, good looks, and sweet words quickly won Karen's heart, and the two were married immediately after graduating from high school.

Undeterred from continuing her education, Karen enrolled in the local community college to take courses during the evening while she worked as a secretary with the city Department of Social Services.

Her marriage to Elroy was very happy in the early years. He attended the police academy, but he always made time for Karen. Soon their first child was on the way. It was joyful news, but it required Karen to quit her job to become a full-time mother and Elroy to accelerate his plans to become a police officer.

The combined pressures of early fatherhood, the rigors of climbing the police department hierarchy, and the responsibilities of providing for a young family put so much strain on Elroy that he began to drink excessively. This destructive pattern progressed to routine physical abuse against Karen. After years of being beaten and harassed, Karen, in the dead of night, while Elroy lay asleep in a drunken stupor, packed her belongings and fled into the night with her son. She was brave enough to try to create a new life.

Starting her life afresh in a new city, Karen assessed her skills to see what kind of work she could pursue. Although she was a fine secretary, she felt it was not her true calling. But art interested her. She remembered that teachers had often remarked on how gifted she was in graphic design. She did it very well and truly enjoyed it. Consequently, she found a job at a small graphic design shop in the downtown area and launched her new career.

While working for this firm during the day, she quietly started her own graphics design business on the side. Karen had the entrepreneurial spirit. She soon generated enough clients to leave her full-time job to cultivate her business.

One reason Karen was able to launch her business so quickly was that she had earned a reputation for appreciating even the smallest things people did for her. If customers turned her down, she would smile and graciously thank them for giving her an opportunity to bid on their business. Despite living in the toughest part of town, she was always cheerful, quick to pass on an encouraging word, and appreciative of the fact that she had a roof over her head, heat in the winter, food to eat, and good health.

Soon, Karen's customers began to notice her positive attitude and unwavering spirit. Although they hadn't given her a lot of business early on, they enjoyed her company because of her gracious spirit.

Karen hoped to build her business so that someday she could hire additional staff, move to a nicer office, and send her son to a private school. But she understood that she had to build upon her current achievements in order to make it to the next level.

About this time one of Karen's prospects called her at home late at night. "Karen, I'm not suppose to tell you this, but we're going to be listing a major contract for graphic design services. I think you can do this work, and the word around the office is that you'd be a great vendor to work with. Although I can't make any promises, I and others here would sure like to see you win. I suggest that you watch the newspaper for the announcement of the bid and put your best proposal forward. Good luck!"

"Thank you so much for the tip, and God bless you," Karen responded.

Karen kept a lookout for the official "Request for Proposal." Two weeks later, the RFP finally hit the street. Karen responded with a well-researched and documented proposal. Although she had minimal resources, she worked overtime and used her special design talent to construct a strong, competitive proposal.

After a long wait and a series of starts and stops, Karen received word that she had been awarded the contract. Soon, she was able to hire five new employees, move to a bright, new office, and buy top-of-the-line computer equipment.

Karen used her positive reputation as leverage when opportunity arose. Even in the face of hardship, she remained undauntedly gracious to those around her. Kindness and a positive outlook were clearly defined assets that Karen valued more than her financial statement.

Wisdom to Take Away

- Average individuals, if asked for an honest personal assessment, would agree that they are not completely content with what they have and where they are in life. Most of us desire bigger and more—a bigger home, a nicer car, a better-paying job, more recognition, enhanced prestige and power. "Constructive discontent" can be good, and indeed it is necessary if entrepreneurs are to push the envelope of opportunity. But if that attitude is allowed to get out of hand, entrepreneurs will lose sight of the wonderful assets they already possess.

- Despite the difficulties of life, all of us are endowed with three types of assets: time, talent, and treasure. All of us are provided with 24 hours in each day to embrace and utilize these assets. All of us have been given certain talents that, when used appropriately, can take us to the top of our particular field or profession. And all of us have more treasures than we realize. These treasures are the "stuff in life." They include not only the things we own, such as our homes, automobiles, bank accounts, stock portfolio, jobs, and businesses, but also our personal relationships.

- To ascend to your next level of success and accomplishment, you must depend upon the assets you possess. In other words, you must first recognize and then leverage your assets effectively. However, you cannot leverage that which you don't value. Consequently, you must value your assets first, then you will be positioned to use them as a stepping-stone to reach greater heights.
- Maintaining a true appreciation of everything you do have also makes the journey to entrepreneurial success less stressful and more enjoyable.

WEEK

2

The Jockey Principle

Sweating the Small Stuff

Andrew could not stop perspiring. As he sat in the lobby of the venture capitalist's office in the swank downtown building, he worried that the sweat would soon soak his finely pressed blue shirt. Being slightly overweight, he was very self-conscious about his appearance. He had been trying for months to arrange a meeting with this particular VC, a man known for his affinity for funding Internet start-ups.

Although Andrew had prepared diligently for this meeting, he still felt a tightness in his gut that he hadn't experienced since his days as an engineering student at Purdue. There, his thoroughness and attention to detail bolstered his achievements, despite the fact that tests often led to nausea and severe stomach cramps. Afraid to look at his exam grades, Andrew would leave his test booklets in a secured school mailbox for days at a time before mustering the courage to review the results. Nevertheless, Andrew graduated from Purdue with honors and embarked on a career as a computer science engineer.

In preparing to the meet with this VC, Andrew had researched the investor. He learned that the firm had considerable capital to invest, but that notwithstanding its interest in technology start-ups, learned that the firm had never backed one owned by an African American. The firm had funded white-owned businesses, female-owned businesses, and Asian-owned businesses. Andrew hoped that prejudice would not be a factor in the outcome of his interview. The possibility, however, made him extremely uneasy.

Andrew set out to do everything he could to impress this gentleman. First, he invested in a new PC and purchased the best business-plan software money could buy. To sharpen his image, he bought an expensive Brooks Brothers suit, a new pair of shoes, and a four-hundred-dollar leather attaché case. As he left his house on the way to the meeting, he inspected himself in the foyer mirror and whispered, "I hope this is the look that will impress these guys!"

"Mr. Saunders, Mr. Villani will see you now." The receptionist beckoned between answering phones.

Andrew made his way into an enormous and ornate conference room. He was impressed by the many plaques and "tombstones" announcing new companies Mr. Villani had invested in that had successfully gone public. Andrew was startled out of his daydream by the abrupt entrance of Mr. Villani and two associates.

Without saying hello, Mr. Villani motioned for Andrew to present his business concept and said that the floor was his. Shaken by the man's abruptness, Andrew shuffled the pages of his business plan. He had assumed that only Mr. Villani would be present and thus had brought only one extra copy. The female associate who had to share appeared insulted at not having her own copy, as she looked over the shoulder of her colleague. They flipped through the business plan that Andrew had painstakingly created.

Feeling a surge of confidence, Andrew transitioned to the heart of his presentation. He started with the business concept for his new dot-com venture and the size of the market. He talked about the operations strategy, the marketing and sales strategies, and the public relations. As he moved to the financial projections and the ultimate exit strategy, Andrew sensed something was wrong. Mr. Villani had not turned to the financials but was still looking at the operations section.

Mr. Villani abruptly closed the business plan, glanced at his watch, and addressed Andrew impatiently. "I see more than one hundred fifty business plans each month. Last year we invested over three hundred million dollars in dozens of new businesses. What makes you special or different? Tell me why I should invest in you."

Andrew turned back to his business plan, but Mr. Villani would not relent. "Mr. Saunders, forget about your presentation and all of your numbers. Tell me why I should invest in *you*. What you fail to understand is that I don't invest in businesses. I invest in people. Over the years, I've learned to bet on the jockey and not on the horse. Now tell me, how good of a jockey are you?"

Andrew was unprepared for this line of questioning, and Mr. Villani realized that Andrew was unable to respond. He ended the meeting and told Andrew that his firm would call Andrew's attorney if he and his associates decided to proceed with the deal.

As the receptionist pointed Andrew to the elevator, he thought about what kind of jockey he really was. He realized he had spent too much time worrying about the horse in the deal instead of focusing on the most critical factor—the jockey. It was not a mistake he would ever repeat. He had a state-of-the-art business plan, and now he would need to spend considerable time planning how to position and present himself as the ideal candidate to run a business.

Wisdom to Take Away

- Becoming a successful entrepreneur requires an acute ability to convince investors, business partners, employees, stakeholders, and customers to believe in you, your product, and your company. To obtain the support and funding of stakeholders, some entrepreneurs rely only on glossy, marketing materials, professionally designed and developed business plans, multimedia presentations, and overly optimistic financial projections. These items may impress some people, but rarely will they impress "money people." Money people are those special individuals who have significant capital to invest and who are experienced investors. Examples of money people would be venture capitalists and "angel" investors.

- Money people have learned that the key to making good investment decisions is to make good *people* decisions. Money people don't invest in businesses or business plans or ideas. Instead they invest in people (the jockeys). They know from experience that they can take an average horse (the business) and an outstanding jockey (the entrepreneur and his management team) and still win the race (accumulation of value in a business investment).

- The secret to becoming an investment-worthy jockey is to get in touch with yourself and your vision for the company. This requires that you spend time each day with your intellectual self, your physical self, and your spiritual self. The intellectual self will tell you what to do. The physical self will provide you the vehicle in which to get it done. The spiritual self will give you peace to understand why you are doing what you do and how your actions fit into the larger plan.

- Only after you've taken care of all three selves will you be at your best and be most competitive. By really knowing yourself and being able to articulate your vision, you can begin to understand your distinctive competence and move closer to making people eager to invest in you.

The Mt. Moosilauke Principle

Government Handcuffs

Sheila loved her job but felt she should be doing more with her life. As a young girl growing up in Richmond, Virginia, Sheila always thought her destiny was predetermined. Having parents who were both career government workers, she assumed her professional life would start and end with the federal government.

Whether it was a self-fulfilling prophecy or the luck of the draw, she did end up working for the government. After a time, she reached a level that allowed her to earn a good salary. She had flexibility in her schedule and could come and go as she pleased. Thus, whenever the children became ill, she could leave work early and tend to their needs. Along with flexibility came the generous benefits package that many government employees enjoy. Tuition reimbursements, liberal health and dental plans, and generous retirement vehicles all served to make her career quite tolerable and in many cases enjoyable.

However, despite these attractive benefits, something was missing from Sheila's life. After months of struggling with this emptiness, she decided to discuss her feelings with her husband, Hank. Over dinner, she started to explain her thoughts. To her surprise, she learned Hank was experiencing similar feelings. He was also a career government employee and had been wrestling with the same problem. That night Sheila and Hank hatched a plan to launch their own nonprofit business.

As they contemplated the specifics, they began to assess what they wanted to achieve, what were they good at, and what need in the community they could collectively meet. The couple decided to provide counseling services to troubled youth. Thus began the Harimbee Counseling Group, Inc. (HCG).

To minimize their risk, Sheila and Hank agreed to build HCG while maintaining their day jobs. Since it was a nonprofit venture, they wouldn't be able to cover their costs for at least the first few months or perhaps a year.

Since they could work on the business only in the evenings and on weekends, their primary challenge was allocating the necessary time for the venture. Then there was the cost of getting their offices established. Although they tried working out of their spare bedroom, it soon became apparent that this was not a long-term option. Between the kids and the increased volume of phone calls, they were forced to invest in office space in the local business park. As their business plan dictated, a major source of funding for their venture would be government and private grants.

Many grants were available for this type of work, but there was also stiff competition. In addition, the time and cost required to complete a grant proposal and application in some cases outweighed the benefit of receiving the grant. The combination of working a full-time day job and building a part-time business at night began to take a toll on Sheila and Hank.

"I feel as if I'm hauling a large boulder up a steep mountain and there's no end in sight." Sheila sighed as she placed the vegetarian casserole on the dining room table.

"I know, honey. I feel the same way," Hank responded. "What's even more frustrating is that our options seem limited. We still haven't gotten the publicity we had hoped for, and so no one really knows about us. Besides, this business is starting to become a cash drain on our family finances. Maybe we should reconsider."

At this juncture, Sheila and Hank knew they had two options. One, they would cut their losses, shut down their operation, and focus on building their careers with the government. Two, they could rethink how they were executing their business plan, intensify their efforts, and fine-tune their strategy to stay on course. They nodded knowingly at each other and smiled. Both understood they weren't ready to give up.

The next week, Hank took a chance and hired a full-time administrative assistant. This move was key because the business could operate during the day when Sheila and Hank were at work. They were able to follow up on more leads and respond to more proposals. Soon their congressman, a friend of a friend, noticed the outstanding work they were doing and invited them to testify before a congressional committee on youth violence. As participants in this congressional inquiry, they met other congressmen and panelists—many of whom expressed a desired to learn more about HCG.

Following the congressional hearing, Sheila and Hank received visitors to observe their program and were being asked to serve on panels and advisory boards. These activities gave them greater contact with influential people, which in turn led to HCG's first major grant.

The funding allowed Sheila and Hank to hire additional staff, become more aggressive in pursuing larger grants, and expand their services to the troubled youth of their city. They built an infrastructure incrementally that supported more opportunities and options. Eventually, Sheila was able to quit her government job to focus on HCG.

As she finished packing up her government office, she thought to herself, "It was tough climbing up the rough side of the mountain, but I'm glad we made the climb."

Wisdom to Take Away

- The process of achieving breakthrough in business is very much like climbing Mt. Moosilauke, a peak in New Hampshire's White Mountains. The Tuck School of Business at Dartmouth College uses the mountain as a team building climbing exercise for its first-year MBA students. The objective is for the class to coalesce as a team and to reach the summit successfully. However, climbing Mt. Moosilauke is no easy feat. First, the journey takes several hours. There is often a 20–30 degree temperature difference between the base of the mountain and its peak. The paths are narrow, slippery, and surrounded by thick brush, so it is difficult to see much until you reach tree line. There, however, you enter a whole new world. Dozens of other footpaths appear that were hidden until you reached the top of the mountain. Without the aid of binoculars, you can see parts of Maine and Vermont, and you become encouraged by the newly discovered paths that offer safer and more navigable options for your descent.
- In the beginning phases of business, your options as an entrepreneur may appear quite limited, and your perception may be that you are forced to operate under tight and unfriendly constraints. Often you are afraid to venture off your designated path for fear of encountering an obstacle that you will be unable to overcome.

- If you can endure to the end, you often will be presented with new opportunities and choices that you
  would have missed had you not taken the journey.
- By plunging into your venture—by giving it all you
  have—you will automatically open up new and exciting opportunities for yourself and your company that
  were initially off of your radar screen. Remember that
  one of the benefits of climbing your entrepreneurial
  mountain is that the effort alone will expand your
  range of choices and entrepreneurial possibilities.

WEEK

4

The 2 X 2 Principle

Waltzing Through the Levels

Stanley found he had a flare for fashion and an affinity for business. In college he earned a reputation as the sharpest dresser on campus. After college, although Stanley accepted a full-time office job, he immediately began working in numerous entrepreneurial endeavors. He had a special interest in multilevel marketing ventures. He would be the first to admit that he never made any money from these opportunities, but they enabled him to make contacts in the business community and learn the ins-and-outs of running a company. Most important, these early experiences helped to put him in the entrepreneurial frame of mind.

Ultimately, he realized he wanted to be in a business he enjoyed and had expertise in. Some self-assessment led him back to his love of clothes and fashion, and the business that resulted focused on clothing designs for Gen-Xers.

Stanley's satisfaction on the job soon began to manifest itself in rapid success. His designs for the hip-hop generation caught on swiftly with both black and Hispanic urban youth and also with young suburban whites and Asians. With sales doubling every year, Stanley built a small but influential fashion business.

During his days as a young entrepreneur, Stanley continued to network and collect new ideas to expand his business intelligence. Every month he enrolled in a class or workshop to sharpen his skills. One workshop was one I hosted based on my book *Black Wealth Through Black Entrepreneurship*. I called the class "Wealth Through Entrepreneurship," and in it I explained the "2 X 2 Principle."

Three tenets undergirded this principle. The first tenet suggested that an entrepreneur must create his own future. By creating a vision of it, Stanley learned he could create a destination—an outcome—toward which all of his efforts could be directed.

The second tenet required that the entrepreneur start at the endpoint and third, break the journey up into incremental pieces or steps and ask, "What must I do to achieve this step?" This process is, in effect, working backward from the destination.

Stanley was hooked by this principle. Although he had achieved some success, he was limited by the constraints he had placed upon his vision for himself and the business. He had limited himself to servicing only the mid-Atlantic region, thinking this market was dynamic enough to sustain his business for some time. But when Stanley was honest with himself, he concluded he had a more encompassing vision.

By using the 2 X 2 principle, Stanley redefined his future. Indeed, he was really striving to be a world-class producer of clothing for young people (the 12–25 age group) and a pacesetter in youth fashions. When he asked the question, "What must I do to achieve this vision?" he identified three tasks: He needed to raise additional capital, expand his marketing focus, and attract new management and skilled workers. With these three new branches leading out of his future vision, he continued to ask the question at the next level: "What must I do to raise additional capital? What must I do to expand my market focus? What must I do to attract managers and skilled workers to my firm?"

When he used the question to expand the branch pertaining to additional capital, he developed three answers: First, he needed to develop viable sources of capital. These sources could conceivably include venture capitalists, banks, private investors, or angel financiers. Second, he needed to revise his financials and his business plan. The new plan had to explain how he would compete on a national and international basis. Third, he needed to define clearly how investors would get their money back and exit from the investment.

Stanley and his team of managers continued to work through the exercise. Only three branches were working their way out of the vision box, but the resulting tree expanded through six levels of iterations and captured dozens of discrete tasks. Stanley integrated each task into his new business plan and began reengineering his business.

With a list of clearly defined tasks, Stanley was able to assign responsibility, target dates, and success criteria for each step that would lead him from his current situation to the vision of what his business could be.

Wisdom to Take Away

- The 2 X 2 principle dictates that in order to achieve certain business objectives (which require planning), you must first create the future (vision) and then work backward.
- When working backward from the vision, it is important to work in a controlled and incremental fashion. At each level, the entrepreneur should ask, "What must I do to achieve the task at hand?" Work diligently to develop at least two answers (see Figure 4.1). These answers then become new nodes in the network of tasks that have to be completed in order to

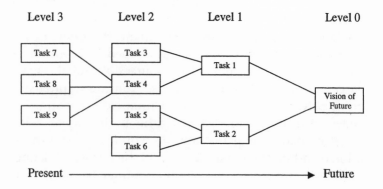

Figure 4.1   The 2 X 2 Principle

make the vision a reality. Continue to ask this same question at each level until you have developed a list of attainable tasks that can be worked on immediately and that will serve to propel you into the future. These attainable and discrete tasks, if defined in a detailed manner, become the building blocks for your business plan.

5

The Principle of
Focused Effort

Breaking Up Is So Hard to Do

"Take this job and shove it—!" Buzz shouted at his now former boss as he stormed around Jerry Alexander's penthouse office. He brusquely knocked a stack of papers to the floor, but in his anger and frustration, he never noticed. "All these years I've worked for this corporation. After all of the money I've earned for you and the stockholders, and this is the appreciation I get! I can do better on my own."

Jerry understood Buzz's anger. He did not respond. He was acutely aware that anything he might say would only fuel this fire.

Almost two weeks later, with no comparable job prospects in sight, Buzz began to wonder if perhaps he had been too quick to react to Jerry's announcement that he was reorganizing the company—and that Buzz would be assuming a lesser role. Jerry said he would take on some of the displaced responsibilities, which did not help soothe Buzz's hurt feelings. Buzz felt betrayed and violated. He had been loyal to the company for eight years and had even turned down other lucrative opportunities to stay in his current job. He now wondered if he had been too loyal.

Jerry had always been kind and generous, although his current actions did not seem to reflect that nature. When Buzz, or Derrick Barron, as he was more formally known, sought employment after completing undergraduate studies at American University, Jerry offered him a position. Buzz might not have broken into his field so soon after graduation if not for Jerry. Buzz cared about his former boss, but not enough to take what he perceived to be a punitive job assignment—indeed, a demotion.

Buzz could not admit that his pride was hurt. Buzz would lose his flexible schedule, since his job entailed international trips to meet with clients. He would lose his expense accounts; even his company car would have to be used sparingly. It all seemed too much like punishment.

Nothing could have been further from Jerry's mind than disparaging or betraying Buzz. He believed in Buzz's uncanny ability to foster trust in clients. When clients wavered about this or that decision, Buzz could make them feel confident in working with the company. The wavering usually ceased after one long lunch with Buzz.

Ten days after Buzz's impromptu resignation, Jerry called. "Hello, Buzz, I know you don't want to talk to me right now, but I need to speak with you." Jerry's voice lacked its usual confidence.

"You've got five minutes, Jerry." Buzz had an idea what Jerry might say, but he didn't want to assume too much.

"I want you to come back to work for me." Buzz could barely hold back a smile.

"Now, Buzz, I think at our last meeting we both said some things we shouldn't have . . ." Jerry wanted Buzz to realize that the disrespect he'd shown his boss had not been forgotten.

"I do apologize, Jerry. It wasn't my intention to insult you. But I have to admit that your announcement stung quite a bit."

Jerry sounded puzzled. "How?"

"When you cut my expenses, my car, and God knows what else, I felt insulted. It was as if everything that I've done for the company didn't matter, Jerry. I know you need me; you know you need me. I've been focusing all my effort on doing a good job for you. Then you cut me back. How else am I supposed to read that?" Buzz felt a heavy weight lift off his shoulders.

"Well, I can say you have been like my right arm since I hired you, Buzz. I am simply concerned about the growth of the business. I was operating only a year before I brought you on board. Now we're experiencing growth, and I think the best way to continue in that vein is if I take on more control, more responsibility."

"More responsibility!" Buzz's temper flared again. But he controlled it to focus on what he wanted to communicate. "You can't give someone a job and take it back without repercussions, Jerry. I'm sorry you feel you don't have enough control, but I honestly don't see how you can manage all that you're taking on."

Buzz thought back to the largest account they'd ever lost. Beakmean Stencils needed them to deliver quickly. Jerry personally took responsibility, but he was involved in so many other time-sensitive accounts that he couldn't give Beakman the attention it deserved. The loss of capital affected the company's third year dramatically.

"What about Beakman, Jerry?" Buzz knew he wouldn't have to say much more than that to stimulate Jerry's memory.

There was a long pause, then Jerry cleared his throat. "Never let me live it down, huh?"

"It's not that, Jerry. It's just that you spread yourself too thin because you didn't trust anybody to handle the account. That's why we lost it. Beakman was our crown jewel until you began a juggling act. We were a team. I can live without some of the perks, but I need to have security in the work I do. I don't want to be second-guessed so you can 'make sure' everything is done. It's my job; it will be done. I will come back to the company if you'll loosen the reins. I know my stuff. It's what you hired me for, remember?"

Two days later, Buzz went back to work for Jerry.

Wisdom to Take Away

- A mistake entrepreneurs commonly make is to try to do too many things at the same time. I term this tendency "opportunity fatigue." The problem is that the entrepreneur spreads himself too thin and ends up doing most things in a mediocre fashion. Since the majority of minority- and female-owned businesses are undercapitalized, there is a natural tendency to take any business that comes their way, even when the new opportunity does not match their core strengths. Taking on more work than you can handle, especially work that is outside your area of expertise, can be deceiving and treacherous.
- Minority and female entrepreneurs also expend resources combating racism and sexism. Many of them can probably recite a list of experiences when they were disregarded, disrespected, or overlooked because of their ethnicity or gender. The reality is that most of us do not have the resources to fight every perceived wrong inflicted upon us. Therefore, we must become proficient at knowing when to "pick our fights" and focus on the things that matter.
- The principle of focused effort suggests that it is better to concentrate on a few tasks and spend the time and

resources to do these tasks exceptionally well. This focus on specialized areas will let you become expert at providing those services. Get your core skills solidified and your key opportunities achieved before expanding into new endeavors.

WEEK

6

The No Man
Is an Island Principle

The Lone Ranger Rides Again

As case number CH18392 in the Department of Social Services database, Denise Graham became very familiar with the City of Seattle's welfare-to-work program. As a single parent of four children, she no longer could provide for her family by herself. It had been easier when she had her husband to help her. However, when he was killed in an automobile accident on the beltway, her life seemed to come to an end.

Unable to meet her and her children's basic needs, she was quickly thrown into the group that economists call the "working poor." In short, she went to work everyday but earned insufficient income to support her family. She had no choice but to turn to the Department of Social Services for welfare assistance.

Raised in the projects by poor but proud parents, Denise had learned to be independent. Rarely would she ask for help from anyone. Even in grade school, Denise took pride in being able to work through her own problems and not depend on anyone for help.

When the Republican Party gained control of the U.S. Congress in 1994 and began dismantling social welfare programs, Denise decided to take charge of her life and open a bookstore. The nation's new "welfare-to-work mantra" forced many welfare recipients to find ways to replace their welfare supplements with other means of income. Denise's fiercely independent attitude made entrepreneurship a likely option. Her small business catered to the reading interests of the African American community.

Starting her own bookstore did not pose a major financial hurdle for Denise. First, it required very little capital up front. She worked the business only in the evenings and on Saturdays and maintained her day job. She rented a retail stall at the local flea market for almost nothing. As for her product, she negotiated deals with local publishers and book distributors to obtain copies of current books on consignment, which enabled her to pay only when they were sold. These arrangements allowed her to manage her cash flow and to have a smaller capital outlay than would normally be expected.

Unfortunately, although the business was well-conceived, Denise's unwillingness to seek informed counsel stymied her efforts almost immediately. There were aspects of business in which she simply had no experience. For example, although her flea-market stall was inexpensive, the location and setup did not attract the kind of customers who had disposable income to spend on books. Thus, she realized very few sales.

Along with misreading the customer, she also ignored the market and technology trends of book publishing. Amazon.com, the darling of Internet stock investors, had revolutionized the merchandising of books, tapes, CDs, and other items. Consumers could go on-line and order books with one click of the mouse. Also, Amazon.com and other large competitors had begun to focus more intensely on books of interest to minorities. Denise was competing against companies she didn't understand because she failed to do the market research.

Depressed about her lack of progress, Denise asked her friend Wayne to join her for a drink and conversation. "You know, Wayne, I was certain this bookstore concept would work. I expected it to be my ticket to success."

Wayne was sympathetic but frustrated, too, with Denise's ongoing refusal to seek expert advice. He knew she was inexperienced in business and had advised her a year ago to meet with a longtime trusted friend who had become a successful business consultant. Unfortunately, her "Lone Ranger" approach locked her into her prescribed course.

Wayne tried again. "Denise, why won't you call my friend Edgar? I'm sure he can help you." Wayne was becoming more impatient with her stubbornness.

"No, I can do this myself. I just need more money and some more time. That's all." Denise set her jaw in that familiar pose. She was stubborn—and there was no changing her mind.

Within a month Denise's company went out of business, and she was left to figure out on her own what had happened and how she would support her struggling family.

Wisdom to Take Away

- Some entrepreneurs perform their duties and tasks like the Lone Ranger. They have the mistaken belief that they can achieve their business objectives by themselves, with little or no help. But even the Lone Ranger needed his friend Tonto every now and then.
- The reality is that true entrepreneurial greatness is realized by working with and through people. The most successful entrepreneurs depend upon assistance from employees, stakeholders, stockholders, suppliers, consultants, and business partners.

- The irony for those who are reluctant to ask for help is that most people who are in a position of power and influence are normally willing to help others. There are some recommended approaches, though, on how to ask for and obtain assistance.

  1. Be humble. Learn to listen to those who are in the know.
  2. Be sure you approach someone who has the experience and the power to help you.
  3. Be specific about what you need help with.
  4. Be prepared to articulate how the individual will personally benefit from helping you. Keep in mind that the benefit need not necessarily be financial.
  5. Learn to set aside your pride. Ask for help.

WEEK
7

The Five Cs Principle

Have Cars, Will Travel

It was a fantastic idea—fast delivery of everything. Michelle and Tyra, two self-titled "regular girls from the 'hood," decided to turn their idea into a business. Both were personable and owned their cars. Michelle Lefferts had a brand-new, shiny black Jeep Cherokee, a graduation gift from her mostly distant father, while Tyra Stuart owned a used and only mildly rusted blue Ford Probe, also a gift, but from her mother. A summer of driving everywhere taught them the expense that cars carry: insurance, repairs, gas, and the like. So they thought it logical to use their vehicles to earn the money that would sustain them. Neither girl had a permanent job. Michelle considered college for a while but decided it wasn't what she wanted. She met Tyra while working at a retail outlet store, and the two became fast friends.

After a little discussion and a lot of planning, M&T Deliveries became reality. The early momentum was curbed, however, when the bank rejected the girls' loan request. The experience briefly dampened their spirits, but they soon regrouped and decided to start gradually and keep overhead low.

Initially, they focused the business on home deliveries. After a time, hoping to grow, they tackled the larger business market. This leap was a fiasco at first—neither knew the ins and outs of delivering time-sensitive material or legal documents. They needed to educate themselves and opted to take part-time jobs with a large delivery service to learn more. The girls' choice to infiltrate the competition was a wise one.

They learned how to increase M&T's productivity with better mapping, a central communications agent, and wireless technology. They were so engrossed that the jobs almost lured them from their own business. Still, they knew when it was time to move on. But because of the earlier loan rejection, the girls wondered if they could attract the capital needed to implement the strategies they were learning.

"It's time we go to a bank and get a loan, 'Chelle." Tyra was insistent.

"Easier said than done, Ty. We tried that in the beginning. Remember? The bank guy looked at us like we had just robbed the place. No more banks." Michelle was afraid of rejection.

After some nudging by Tyra, they arrived at another bank with all of their hopes neatly organized in a manila envelope filled with document, records, credit ratings, and testimonials promising that they would be trustworthy loan candidates

The loan officer, Ms. Sanders, was kind. She had a gracious smile and a manner that put one at ease. "Well, ladies, what kind of loan are you looking for?" Her question made them uncomfortable. They were unfamiliar with the various loan options that existed.

"Ma'am, we are interested in a small loan to expand our business." Tyra was direct, though her knees shook.

"And how much were you looking to borrow?" Ms. Sanders beamed hope at them.

"About thirty-six thousand dollars." They had projected that figure would allow them to hire other drivers with experience. It also would provide them a more legitimate location, since they currently worked out of Michelle's apartment with Tyra's cellphone.

"Do you have collateral?" The question they expected.

"Yes, we own two automobiles at this blue book value." Michelle freed a sea of papers from the manila folder. As she pored over them, Ms. Sanders commented on their unusual but organized style of recordkeeping. She also found more than enough evidence to approve their loan.

"Ladies, you could have obtained this loan long ago. This bank survives by collaborating with honest people like you who want to improve their homes or businesses. Congratulations."

Michelle and Tyra were elated. They didn't regret not having sought a loan sooner. After all, the delay had given them the time and opportunity to learn more about the delivery business and to gain the professional experience that prepared them to spend the newly provided capital wisely.

Wisdom to Take Away

- An unfair reality of doing business in America is that minority and female entrepreneurs often get only one chance to impress a customer or a group of investors. Some investors are especially unforgiving in their assessment of the value and validity of entrepreneurs and their ideas. To increase your chances of winning a customer or an investor's favor, remember these five Cs:

    Character: Moral excellence and firmness
    Capacity: Ability to repay what has been borrowed
    Collateral: What the investor can seize if you don't deliver

Capital: Cash, Stocks, Bonds, or any liquid asset resources (usually money) you are willing to put "at risk"

Credit: Repayment history and level of trustworthiness

- When approaching investors about committing capital to your venture, be sure to prepare answers to the following questions prior to meeting:

  1. How much capital will you need?
  2. How will investors be repaid or "made whole"?
  3. How will the capital be used?
  4. What collateral can be used to repay the loan if the project fails?

WEEK
8

The Principle of
Dream Embodiment

The Dream Girl

At 5 A.M. the alarm announced daybreak for Lucita. A three-mile run, a nutritious breakfast, and a little morning praise and worship began her usual day before she reported to the office. But this day was different because of a dream she had the night before. She dreamed in rich, vivid color. She could feel and smell and hear and see everything.

In her dream, Lucita Maldonado, the shy Dominican girl from Brooklyn, was at the helm of a thriving import-export business. She enjoyed the admiration of her colleagues, friends, and family. Dressed in beautiful clothes with a personal assistant scribbling her every word, Lucita had become the success story she always dreamed of. Just as her assistant announced her personal masseur, a rippling and well-oiled Miguel, she woke up. What timing.

The dream left her unsettled yet exhilarated. She could scarcely remember parts of it and wondered about its significance. As details came to her, it started to make sense. She had been dreaming about her hobby. For three years she'd been bringing beautiful little artifacts and art pieces home for friends and relatives on her frequent trips to see her maternal grandmother, her Dia. Her family in the Dominican Republic was well-to-do, so she never paid for lodging or airfare. She often wondered if she could build a thriving business around her love of Dominican crafts and art.

Though the dream was just a dream, it lingered. On the bus to work, Lucita peered out the window, transported by the imagery of the dream. The success, the benefits of the success, and the sense that she deserved it were irresistibly intoxicating elements in her fantasy.

Her workday passed uneventfully until noon. Three coworkers nabbed her for lunch and some window-shopping. Heather, Chou Li, and Sally ordered salads at the local Salad-O-Rama, while Lucita lapsed into her trance again.

"Hey, hey, anybody in there?" chimed Heather, rousing Lucita from her dreamlike state.

"Sorry, I just had this dream last night and . . . "

"So tell," coaxed Chou Li.

Lucita told them in detail about her dream. "I can't help thinking it was a sign," she concluded.

"Sign, shmign. It was a dream. I dream about being a ninja warrior so I can chop my husband down when he gets out of line. Hy-ah!" Chou Li cut the air with a karate chop. She loved to mimic the American perception of Asians. "Dreams tell us about how we feel now. They aren't meant to tell the future."

"I can't explain exactly how I feel. In my dream I was a great lady—just like my Dia. I think the dream somehow means more than I'm grasping."

Sally struggled to suppress a laugh attack at Lucita's expense. "Seriously, Lucy, if you dream of being an entrepreneur, then do it. It's worth the risk. My mom dreamed about being a beautician when she was young, and her effort has paid off for her."

Lucita only half heard the attempt at encouragement from Sally because she had glimpsed something as compelling to her as the dream. A well-dressed Hispanic woman who resembled the dream version of Lucita but perhaps ten years older, was exiting a limousine with assistants in tow attending to her needs. The mystery lady pointed to some reference in a book, her hand movements—accentuated by the glimmer reflecting off of a large rock. The scene was much like her dream. But this was reality. Lucita felt inspired as never before. Her friends, busy chatting, didn't even notice the woman.

Before they returned to the office, Heather pulled Lucita aside. "Look, most people dream of great things, but it never happens. I don't want to see you disappointed. When was the last time you saw someone like us working stiffs draped in success and diamonds?"

Lucita, no longer concerned about being disappointed, had already resolved to quit her job and take the plunge. She laughed. It was about time.

Wisdom to Take Away

- Dreams are the forces that help keep us alive. Usually entrepreneurs who have passion, energy, and drive in their ventures are motivated by a compelling dream. Whether they dream of opening a mom-and-pop corner store or an e-commerce business, dreams of success are the first step toward reality.
- Inspiration is vital. When we see a dream come true for another human being, the dreams we have for ourselves seem attainable. Where would many of today's most successful people be if not for the trails blazed by others?

WEEK
9

Removing the Power of the Stake Principle

The Circus

Springtime was always exciting for young Taylor Kimble. With its bright sunshine, blooming flowers, and longer days, spring was her escape from winter doldrums. Spring was also a delightful time because it brought the pageantry and spectacle of the circus to town.

Few experiences delighted Taylor more than the excitement and glamour of the circus. She especially marveled at the acrobats, the clowns, and the wild animals—each a major component in the whimsy and magic. From the time she was eight, she could remember the many annual encounters with the enchanting visitors from the east. In later years, she would recall with fondness the seemingly endless caravan of lions, monkeys, tigers, and elephants supported by the bright yellow and orange circus wagons used to parade these sometimes unwilling participants down Main Street. She would firmly clutch her father's hand as she pushed through the crowd to get a better glimpse of the parade.

Taylor marveled at the big, intimidating, yet deceptively gentle elephants. There seemed to be a passivity about them that didn't fit their stature, strength, and physical dominance. As the ringmaster led the family of elephants into the tent, they calmly followed his commands and moved into their assigned positions without disruption.

During the circus performance, Taylor noticed that while the ringmaster was working with some of the elephants, the others outside of center ring were tied by a long, thin, rusty, chain to a stake in the ground. The chain seemed inadequate to hold these giant animals. Yet the elephants stood quietly and docilely connected to the small stake in the ground.

As Taylor grew older, the image of the powerful elephant being held in check by a rusted chain and a tiny steel stake didn't make sense. One particular day of the circus, sitting at center ring as always, Taylor tugged at her father's sweater and inquired about the status of her favorite animals. "Daddy, the elephants look so sad tied up to that little pole in the ground. They look so much bigger and stronger than that chain and stake. Why don't they just yank the stake out of the ground and do what they want to do?"

Her father, moved by her care and respect for animals, replied, "Well, sugar, the elephant trainer spends a long time training the elephants to be obedient and to do what they're told to do. He takes the elephants when they are very young and conditions them to follow his every command." Taylor locked onto his words intently.

"One important lesson he must teach the elephants is that they must obey and respect the stake in the ground. They are trained that when they are tied to the stake, they must stay attached to it and not attempt to pull away. So even as the elephants grow up to be big, strong, and powerful creatures, they have been taught to respect the stake and its power."

Taylor stared at her daddy for a long time, then abruptly turned her gaze toward the chained elephants. A wrinkle of confusion and sadness creased her forehead. "Do you mean that if the elephants wanted to, they could break the chain or pull the stake out of the ground?"

"Yes, sugar, that's exactly right. All they have to do is make a choice to pull the stake up to realize that it has very little power on its own against them."

Surprised by these unexpected facts about the elephants. Taylor leaned back in her seat and whispered to herself, "The elephants look so tired and sad. I hope one day they decide to pull the stake out of the ground and run away so that they will be happy."

Taylor went on to become the first at many things: first black woman on full scholarship at her university, first black executive at a prestigious law firm, even first woman to found an organization for the homeless. These were among her many accomplishments. Taylor had understood the power of the stake from that day at the circus—and she never forgot it. More important, she learned that she was able to exercise her own power and that the stake was just a stake.

Wisdom to Take Away

- The typical entrepreneur, in a moment of weakness, is reminded of some form of a sharp, deep, stake that firmly keeps them in "their place." For some, this stake is racism and bigotry. They have concluded that they are the "wrong" color and therefore cannot achieve true success. For others, this stake may be sexism. Women feel that their gender automatically renders them uncompetitive. For many more entrepreneurs, the stakes that fasten them tightly in place may be age, weight, height, culture, or religion. The worst-case scenario is that too many stakes often mean certain failure.

- Usually the stake has no inherent power. The stake has only as much power as the entrepreneur allows. For instance, you could let the stake of sexism dictate what opportunities you try to capitalize on, but then you will be afraid to attempt things that are rarely accomplished by women. By focusing on the stake, you automatically divert to it your power, energy, and ability to perform. It is prudent to recognize that the stake exists—and then to recapture the power it appears to possess by assuming full ownership of your destiny.

Recapturing the
Dead Zone Principle

The Dissatisfied Banker

"You've done it again, DeLois!" the customer said to the young owner of the Centennial Mortgage Company. "Every year you guys put on the finest holiday celebration in the city. I always look forward to attending."

Bob Crandle was a valued Centennial customer, so his comments made DeLois Stafford smile. "Thank you so much, Bob. This is simply our way of saying thanks to customers like you who have supported us throughout the year. You are very important to us, and I'm grateful for the relationship we have established." DeLois always had the appropriate response delivered warmly.

In reality, however, the Christmas party was the furthest thing from her mind. Her mortgage business had made strides during the year, but DeLois felt her company could have prospered more had she done things differently. Although her partners felt she was being too hard on herself, she took personal responsibility for what she regarded as her own lackluster performance. No matter how she scrutinized the past years, she always concluded that she was not operating at her best.

After extending warm holiday wishes to the last customer to arrive at the gathering, she tipped the caterer and thanked him for his outstanding service, jumped into her silver BMW, and began the long ride home. DeLois could not smile anymore.

At the outset, DeLois had understood that the mortgage business was highly competitive. Consequently, she had to be at the top of her game every single day in order to survive. She applied her homegrown discipline to the challenge. Her day routinely started at 5:30 a.m. when she checked the new mortgage rates and tried to position her clients to take advantage of any new developments in the industry. By 7:30 she was normally hitting her stride, deeply immersed in critical business activities.

As each day progressed, she began to notice so many other business issues that required her attention but that added little value to the firm and even less to the bottom line. She was continually sidetracked. Office operations, material ordering, furniture selection, and vendor payments began to consume more of her time. By the end of the day, she was exasperated and fatigued.

To compensate, she routinely brought her work home in the evenings to finish there. The arrangement seemed logical. She could spend time with her family, then use any extra time to develop her business. But by the time she finished making dinner for her husband and two little boys, she was physically exhausted. She shifted to "autopilot" as the time between dinner and putting the children to bed was spent helping the children with their homework, after which she collapsed in front of the television set. She had no time to spend on herself as a person, as a woman, as an entrepreneur. She could see how so many men without her household responsibilities had done better throughout the years.

She was burned out. Having so much responsibility at home and at work meant she couldn't really focus on either. It was a never-ending circle; something had to change. The new year would be different.

When January 1 rolled around, DeLois sought the advice of a close friend who specialized in time management. This expert's first advice was that DeLois inventory how she spent her time during a typical day. She immediately began documenting in detail all of the meetings, planning, phone calls, emergencies, and staff management that occupied most of her day. She was horrified to find that she was spending nearly 80 percent of her time "putting out fires" and performing tasks that were not adding any value to the business.

Realizing these inefficiencies, DeLois made some changes. First, she became more aggressive at delegating administrative and routine tasks to her assistants and business partners. For every request she received, she would ask herself, "Who in my organization is qualified to handle this matter?" She would immediately pass it on to that person and ask her assistant to follow up on the activity and report to her the status or completion date.

DeLois also took action at home. She hired a part-time housekeeper to meet her children at the bus stop, help them with their homework before DeLois returned home, and prepare dinner for her family. These new arrangements enabled DeLois and her husband to spend quality time with each other and with their children.

Improved efficiency also gave DeLois more time in the evenings to concentrate on strategic items that directly impacted her business. Ideas generated under these conditions seemed more thought out and focused. She was amazed at how productive she was. Her discipline paid off the way it had so many times before.

As the year progressed, DeLois saw her effectiveness reflected in business results—they exceeded everyone's expectations. To celebrate the year's performance, the company moved its annual Christmas party to a big hotel downtown and expanded the invitation list. As she and her business partners greeted their customers, her favorite customer made his way to the front of the line.

"Hello, Bob. Welcome back again to our party. It's so nice to see you."

"Nice to see you again, DeLois. I trust you had an outstanding year."

DeLois smiled. "We had a marvelous year, thanks to customers like you and my ability to recapture the dead zones of my day. Filling in those dead zones with productive activity has made a difference in my business and in my life."

DeLois kept many of her male customers busy on the dance floor most of the night.

Wisdom to Take Away

- The "dead zone" is that block of time in an entrepreneur's day that is completely unproductive. It can occur at any time of day or night.
- Entrepreneurs who are attempting to move their business to the next level may find it necessary to recapture this dead zone and turn it into a productive period. Don't stress. Allow your thinking to evolve naturally.
- The first step in recapturing the dead zone is to monitor your tasks over a few days. Track your time to see at what part of the day you are most and least productive. After isolating the unproductive patterns, develop strategies that will allow you to make this time more productive. Concurrently, try to accomplish all critical tasks during the period you are most productive.

11

The Principle of Perpetual Self-Validation

Homecoming

Gilbert reclined contentedly next to the sparkling blue pool sipping on his Coke, the bright Florida sun reflecting off his mirrored sunglasses. He had decided to take a short vacation with his family just after closing the biggest deal of his career—worth millions! It was by far the largest deal his firm had ever negotiated. Although his information-technology consulting firm had only 25 employees at the time, they had competed for and ultimately won a large consulting contract from a major east coast city. The success was even sweeter because they had competed against the "big boys"— Anderson Consulting, KPMG, Booze Allen & Hamilton, and IBM. The proverbial David had slain the giant Goliaths.

Gilbert took another cool sip from his drink as his son Kyle climbed out of the pool to dry off in the shade of the tall, lush palm tree. Gilbert motioned to his son to join him at poolside.

"You still thinking about the deal you just won?" Kyle asked as he relaxed in the lounger next to his dad.

"How'd you know?" Gilbert began to reflect on the events that led up to his successful bid. "You know, son, during the twelve-month sell cycle on that deal, there was every indication that we were never going to win the business. We were really competing against the big boys. They had all of the advantages—bigger, more experienced, more resources, and in some cases a long-term relationship with the customer. It would have been easy for us to give up and convince ourselves that we didn't have a chance of winning."

The experience reminded Gilbert of his freshman year in college. He recounted the story to his son:

"I was seventeen and in my first year at Stanford and was ecstatic about living on the west coast and being out on my own. I was brimming with self-confidence as I prepared for what I knew would be tough classes in mechanical engineering and applied mechanics. I had finalized my schedule and was told to meet with my academic adviser, Dr. Zhandi, and get his approval of my course selections for the semester. Well, my first encounter with Dr. Zhandi was not a good one. After reviewing my schedule, he impatiently snorted at me, 'Mr. Sanchez, I doubt very seriously that you'll make it here at Stanford's School of Engineering!'

"'I don't believe this fool,' I thought to myself. 'He's supposed to be on my side, my mentor, and my adviser. Why is he destroying my confidence before I've begun my studies? Didn't he read my high school records? Didn't he know that I had studied my way to a 3.8 grade point average and had earned varsity letters in four sports?' I was shocked and humiliated. In that brief instant I had let this man destroy all the confidence that it had taken me seventeen years to build. I backed down.

"After Dr. Zhandi's damaging assessment of me, I angrily left the room. I dashed down the dark, gray halls of the engineering school, sprinted across the courtyard, and darted up to my dorm room. I was careful to pull my hat down over my face to hide the tears I couldn't hold back. I was devastated. As I opened the door to my room, I suddenly felt a need to hide. I ran to the corner of the room between my bed and my desk and squatted there, sobbing uncontrollably. Day gave way to night as I remained in the corner.

"By dawn I had convinced myself that I was not good enough to study engineering at Stanford. Bitter and demoralized, I summoned the courage to call Momma and Daddy to ask their permission to come home. To my relief, Momma was the first to answer the phone.

"'Hi, baby. Are you getting all set up there at that school?'

"I swallowed, took a deep breath, and said, 'Momma, I want to come home.'

"Momma replied, 'What's wrong, son? Are they treating you all right?'

"'No, Momma, they're not. I want to come home.'

"Momma said quietly, 'I think you'd better talk to your daddy.'

"I dreaded having to talk to Daddy in this situation. But in seconds he was talking to me. 'Son, your mother tells me you want to come home. How can that be when you haven't even started classes yet?'

"'Dad, my adviser thinks I'm not good enough to be here, and you know, maybe he's right.'

"There was a long silence on the other end of the phone. My daddy was a man of great deliberation, deep thoughts, but few words. Finally he spoke, and what he said has stuck with me and helps keep me together to this day.

"Daddy bellowed, "Boy, your momma and I have worked long and hard to get you into that university. Everyone in this family has made a sacrifice for you to have this opportunity. You are our first to attend college, and I'm not going to let you tuck your tail and run at the first sign of trouble. You're better than that, so start acting like it! You're talking like a loser and a chump, and don't forget, boy, I didn't raise no chumps. So you'd better get your self up, dry your eyes, and get ready for your classes. We'll talk again at the end of the semester, and don't be calling here worrying your momma. Good-bye!'

"I was frightened, humbled, but focused. I started attending classes, reflecting on Daddy's words daily. I studied that semester as I had never studied before. Every time I saw Dr. Zhandi, his presence only served to make me stronger. It got so I looked forward to seeing him just so he would know I hadn't given up. At the end of that semester I triumphantly called Daddy to tell him I had made the dean's List.

"You know, Kyle, the Dr. Zhandi episode was constantly in my mind during this contract bidding. Once again someone was saying that we couldn't successfully compete. I saw his arrogant smile as we sought to prove to the city our technical capability. It's always sweet to win a contract, but knowing we won this one because we're good and believed in our collective strength and ourselves makes this victory even sweeter."

Wisdom to Take Away

- Regardless of how accomplished entrepreneurs may think they are, there will always be someone who questions their competence. Some successful entrepreneurs believe that your potential for success is directly proportional to the number of doubters you encounter. Nevertheless, the challenge for you as an entrepreneur is to determine whether you will view these situations as motivators or as insurmountable impediments.
- Using challenges as a motivator requires constantly being in touch with yourself and your strengths. Self-validation provides the impetus to stay engaged. When others challenge you, use your prior successes as a source of strength.

12

The Principle of Failure

The Reluctant Programmer

Wayne Simmons spent years studying to become a top-notch Web engineer and developer. He paid attention to every detail of his education and career path from the schools he attended to the technical experiences he added to his repertoire of projects. He won his first computer in a competition at his high school. It turned out to be more of a toy than the high-tech machines he dealt with today.

Wayne's reputation for professionalism, creativity, honesty, and trustworthiness was an asset in the Internet and information-technology consulting fields. Although many of his peers and competitors routinely cut corners, Wayne remained steadfast in always doing what was right and best for his clients.

Because of his reputation, Wayne found it easy to maintain a pipeline of contracts and business opportunities for himself and his growing consulting firm. One such opportunity took him to south Florida to oversee a major Web development project for Mantchell, Inc., a multibillion-dollar corporation. This was the first such effort initiated by the company; thus the project was expected to receive close scrutiny from senior executives as well as from outsiders in the industry.

Phyllis Wyles, Mantchell's vice-president in charge of the project and the company's chief technology officer, had worked with Wayne years before when he was a manager at Bell Laboratories. Even then she was impressed with his intelligence and trustworthiness and was comfortable working with him. As the work at Bell Labs reached completion, Phyllis terminated her contract with Bell to accept a position at Mantchell. She promised Wayne she would keep in touch and would bring him into bigger and even more exciting technical opportunities when she became situated.

True to her word, Phyllis kept in touch with Wayne no matter where he relocated. Finally, the two had connected on the opportunity to work together on the Florida project.

Wayne was assigned to be the project manager for a team of five Web programmers. Their work for Mantchell was actually being primed by another company out of Chicago, and Wayne as a subcontractor was required to send his team's billable hours to the prime's accounting department every two weeks. The accounting department would then compile all of the labor hours and submit one integrated invoice to the client. None of these details mattered to Wayne at the time because he was focused on the team's project. In fact, he rarely glanced at the hours being billed. However, his lack of attention to these details would soon come back to haunt him.

Wayne's work was progressing so well that the client requested that Wayne, his manager, and a representative from the programming staff fly to Chicago to give a briefing. Without hesitation the trio booked flights on the next Monday morning shuttle.

Feeling confident and eager to discuss the project, Wayne put the finishing touches on his presentation in his hotel room that evening. He rehearsed his part of the next day's meeting over and over and considered several scenarios. As he pondered the multiple possibilities, he soon dozed off into much-needed sleep.

The next morning, feeling vibrant and full of energy, Wayne met up with Craig Ramos, his manager, and Susan Nguyen, his Web programmer, and they made their way to the fifteenth-floor offices of the client's lakeside offices.

As Wayne and Susan set up their laptops for their presentation, the client and his team entered the room and took their assigned seats. Craig readied the data sheets per the agenda. They were ready to start.

Mantchell, Inc. was impressive. It projected a showy image with its exotic African and Asian artwork and statuary. Even the conference room was designed as an amphitheater with state-of-the-art equipment. Wayne surveyed the setup approvingly; it was sure to showcase his presentation in the most positive light.

His mood darkened, however, when he perused the financials distributed by the client. Moments passed like hours as he rechecked the project synopsis. He was shocked to discover a mistake in the workload report that made the presentation results questionable. His presentation would reflect three programmers, but the report (which showed actual billed hours) clearly listed five programmers plus Wayne, which made six on the payroll.

Wayne knew the revenues had been reported incorrectly. They had been overbilling the client since the project started, and Wayne had never realized it until today.

Wayne faced a major dilemma. If he told the client that, yes, he had six programmers on the project, he would be lying. If he admitted the truth, he would immediately lose all of the credibility he had spent so much time building.

Finally, Wayne looked across the table at the client and in a calm and direct voice explained the error. Wayne hoped his admission would be met with understanding. It wasn't.

"Wayne, I'm really disappointed in this. It will take months to fix this fiscally," Phyllis barked at him. She was obviously embarrassed, since she had acted as the liaison. Wayne couldn't blame her.

Gordon Hilliman, one of the executive officers, rose from his chair. He spoke with great haughtiness. "We have no time for this type of mistake. As such, your presentation is moot, and this meeting is moot."

With that, the executives filed out the door. Only Phyllis turned around. "Wayne, call me about this later, okay?" He nodded.

Wayne was unable to speak from that moment until he returned to his hotel room. This was his first real failure. He hadn't correctly managed an important facet of the job, and it would almost certainly cost him future business. Tomorrow he would need to formulate a plan to rectify the problem and learn from his failure.

Wisdom to Take Away

- Business statistics indicate that, on average, entrepreneurs fail between five and seven times in business before they stumble into ventures that ultimately lead them to success. Failure is an integral part of the process of becoming successful. You cannot achieve true success until you have experienced some level of failure. Fortunately, each failure provides an opportunity for you to learn more about your character insufficiencies, strategic and tactical flaws, and adequacy of work execution. Once the weaknesses are identified, the plan to remedy the situation can be put in motion.
- Failure makes successes more enjoyable. Tasting the embarrassment and pain of failure makes the sunshine of success brighter.

- When faced with failure, as all successful entrepreneurs ultimately are, you must decide whether to allow the failure to destroy you or use it instead to motivate and empower. Remember that failure is neutral. It can be your best friend or your worst enemy. Which companion do you want it to be?

WEEK

13

The Getting There by Starting Where You Are Principle

Opportunity Knocks

The final boxes had been delivered to the storeroom, and Mandy Cellers was pleased with herself for a number of reasons. She'd overcome fear to launch her own showroom for luxury items on Manhattan's Upper West Side. The rent was astronomical, but she'd saved enough and borrowed enough to stay afloat for a while. She anticipated attracting a clientele through contacts she had already made.

Still, there was additional work to be completed before she could open the doors. She needed at least a few weeks to get the store in order. Collin, a friend from college, advised her to get started right away to avoid losing money on the rent. She had opted instead to set herself a three-week deadline. The store had to be perfect. It needed to be put together with care or not at all. She wasn't going to be like so many others who rush to get started only to find no business to tend to but endless chores left unfinished.

Hidden Treasures was targeted at high-net-worth clients. She was selling eclectic items such as one-of-a-kind Italian boots, first editions of Twain, Poe, and Shaw, rare fragrances, and unique pottery. She believed her boutique items could bring a quick return. Competition in the area was sparse. Many neighboring stores sold high-ticket clothing or specialty foods. Her showroom was an ideal match for the neighborhood. Even better, she set up a Web site to attract orders via the Internet. She had the right idea, the right location, and the right stock. Now all she needed was more time in the day.

Two weeks whizzed by and the store was ahead of schedule. Mandy could have opened but wanted to use the remaining week to line up some additional public relations for opening day. One early afternoon, the front bell sounded. At the door was a small woman smoking a long brown cigarette through a six-inch holder. Swathed in rich browns and smoky grays, she peered through the glass door.

"Sveetie, sveetie! Open up!" She sounded eastern European.

"Can I help you with something , ma'am?"

"Ve have movie next block. You open up. Let us buy vhat ve need."

She sounds like Natasha from *Rocky and Bullwinkle*, Mandy thought. "The store isn't open yet. Next week. Sorry."

Before Mandy could close the door, the woman pushed her way in and stormed the imported boot rack. "Perfect! Perfect! How much?"

Pleased with the compliment on her taste yet appalled at the woman's lack of tact, Mandy tried to be accommodating yet firm. "I'm afraid you misunderstand. The store will not be open until next week." She wanted to stay on plan.

The woman locked her eyes on Mandy and smiled sweetly. "You have store. Store sells things, yes?"

"Yes."

"I have money. Movie needs things. You have store. America is wonderful country, no?"

"No, I mean yes," Mandy stammered. She couldn't help being tempted by the opportunity to make her first lucrative sale. And for a movie!

"Sveetie, I need to get back. Boots, yes? Oh, and this vase? How much?" The woman was relentless.

"Eight hundred." Mandy covered her mouth after saying it. She couldn't believe she was going to sell this woman the vase and the boots a week before opening. She was abandoning her plan to delay sales until the store was finished. The woman paid cash and promptly left.

Mandy went into the storeroom and laid the money out in front of her. She was puzzled and thrilled and perplexed. Did it matter how much she'd planned for an opening when business was available now?

It was only a few minutes before she made the necessary calls to suppliers, friends, and family who promised to help out and move their schedules up a few days. The next morning, Natasha returned with one of the film's actors and a producer. Within a couple of hours, they had lined up personal purchases, catalog orders, and prop purchases that would keep Mandy profitable for weeks.

That night, Mandy reflected on the past two incredible days. She had learned so much about business in such a short time. Most important, a knock from opportunity is usually a surprise—and one worth answering.

Wisdom to Take Away

- Successful entrepreneurs lead lives full of continuous tension between the present and the future. These special people are grateful for what they have achieved, but they are always striving to do more, get more, and be more. However, they understand that to get to the future, they must start with the present.

- Some people are under the mistaken assumption that "the grass is always greener . . . ." This observation may or may not be true, but efficiency dictates that you must start the journey to your future from where you stand today.
- Don't wait until some special event has occurred before you start taking action to achieve your stated objectives. The future happens the moment you act. For example, don't wait until your firm's revenues reach a certain level before you attempt to seek out larger and more diverse clients. Go after them now. Don't wait until you move to a bigger, nicer office before you hire more staff. Start the hiring process now. Whatever you deem the appropriate next steps, don't delay; start where you are and move forward.

PART TWO

Principles of Building Entrepreneurial Success

WEEK
14

The Breakthrough
("First Hit") Principle

Swooning Tunes

Cary and Sandy Bruner were mirror images of each other. From the womb, the twins learned to share, to balance, and to synthesize. They played the usual games of "switch" on family and friends. Once, Cary convinced their father that she was Sandy in order to receive an extra allowance. She figured Sandy wouldn't mind, because she had planned to use her ill-gotten gains to purchase records the two wanted. Their shared love of music had already resulted in an extensive collection of valuable 78s and 33s, purchased over the years and received as gifts on birthdays and Christmas.

They began by finding rare Bessie Smith and Billie Holiday recordings at the garage and estate sales their mother frequented. Usually, Sandy would find and choose the records while Cary haggled over the price. By their last month of high school, they had attracted the attention of shrewd collectors and were receiving frequent offers— sometimes unfair offers designed to cheat them—to buy the entire anthology. One fellow collector, Jack Quinlan, made an especially low offer and insisted it was a fair price.

He assumed they were naive. The girls, insulted and surprised, never forgot the experience.

The girls ultimately decided to use their collection as collateral to secure a loan for a small retail business specializing in antique recordings.

The first ten months in business were brutal. The twins, usually the best of friends, squabbled over marketing and customer retention. They loved to collect—but had a lot yet to learn about business. Cary managed to land a few regular accounts through their Web page, but these weren't sufficient to maintain a steady level of business. The girls sensed the urgency: Their bank loan would support only eighteen months of the venture. The remaining capital would need to come directly from sales.

Although nervous, they persevered. Their lucky break, it turned out, came at an estate sale in New Haven, Connecticut, and from a very unexpected source—their old business nemesis, Jack Quinlan.

Cary and Sandy were about to leave the sale, a few new items in hand, when Sandy spotted him. She grabbed Cary, pulling her close. "Hey, wait! Isn't that the man himself? Isn't that Quinlan over there?"

Sure enough, there was Quinlan. Almost at the moment she saw him, he turned and locked eyes with the twins. He brightened and headed toward them with a cheery wave of his hand. Sandy planted her feet and tightened her vice grip on Cary's arm.

"What are you doing here, Quinlan?" Sandy barked. "I'm surprised to see you on the legitimate circuit. No more innocent children's dreams left to squash?"

"Now I don't think I deserve that, miss. I realize that our first meeting was a little strained."

"Whatever. So, I hear you recently sold a chunk of your collection. Business bad?" Cary interjected.

"Hardly. I decided to quit. I've grown tired of the constant competition. I'm merely here to help the executor, a dear friend of mine. Listen, ladies, I want you to know that I meant you no harm. If there's anything I can do. . . ." Quinlan seemed sincere, as if all those years of haggling had somehow led to a change of heart.

Sandy was ready to lash out again when Cary was struck with a better idea and took her sister aside.

"Listen, Sandy, we could use this moment to make an invaluable contact. If Quinlan is out of the business, maybe he'll be willing to give us some advice. We could use the help. So he tried to get a low price from two kids. Is that any different from the time you convinced Grandma Ruthie's best friend Carol, the woman with cataracts, that all her Jolson recordings were her grandson's Earth Wind and Fire albums?"

Sandy, at first resistant to the idea of trusting Quinlan, eventually agreed. In a mere five minutes, they convinced Quinlan to serve as a consultant for their store for a very nominal fee—gratitude.

Thanks in part to Quinlan's counsel and support, the next several years saw a significant growth spurt in the business. The twins eventually made Quinlan a partner, and their surprising experience taught them much about the road to success, including forgiveness.

Wisdom to Take Away

- Entrepreneurs who have a good idea and the resolve to see it through will experience an event called the "first hit," or breakthrough, point. This event could be a chance encounter. It could also be winning a strategic contract or skillfully handling a difficult and volatile situation under the watchful eye of a prospective client. After this breakthrough point, good things begin to happen—the business turns a corner. Not only do sales increase, but the business also begins—if managed properly—to grow at a steady pace thereafter.

- For an entrepreneur beginning a venture, there are typically two performance curves of concern: the *investment curve* and the *return curve*. The investment curve represents what you put into the venture, time, money, etc. And the return curve represents what you get back. Returns can be either measurable like profits, net income, net worth, and price/earnings ratio or intangible. These immeasurable returns include prestige, power, reputation, influence, and credibility. At the beginning of the venture, the investment is high and the results are at zero. Although you are making major contributions to the venture, it is too early in the process to realize any significant returns.
- The breakthrough point is when momentum picks up, and the return and investment curves intersect. The investment is going down and moving toward zero, and the return curve is going up and moving toward infinity. At any time beyond the breakthrough point you will enjoy more benefits from the venture than what you are investing.
- Every entrepreneur's objective must be to get to that breakthrough point. Unfortunately, many entrepreneurs give up just before they reach it. As always, exercise prudence in your journey, but be careful not to give up too early.

WEEK
15

The Bucket Principle

Twice As Nice

Everyone was proud of Malcolm Jones. At fifteen, he saved three children from a fire. At nineteen, he published his first book of poetry. At twenty-three, he organized a local community center in his hometown of Reston, Virginia. He married his college sweetheart, Rachel. Four times he was elected to head the town council. Yet, all the success he enjoyed was sometimes overshadowed by his consuming obsession: his new wilderness supply store.

His first store, Jones & Jones Camping Supply, was performing well, far exceeding his projections, even turning a tidy profit at the end of the year. J&J Supply, the spin-off, however, was beginning to drain his revenue with no end in sight.

Each morning brought the richness of the sunrise stretched into rays of magenta, pale gold, and purple. It also brought a pang of despair because of the failing business. Mal could barely gather the strength to begin the usual routine of opening both locations, a chore he once enjoyed.

As he trudged downstairs to breakfast one morning, he found Rachel preparing a feast of his Sunday favorites: blueberry waffles from scratch, sausage, eggs, fried apples, juice, coffee, and fresh biscuits. This was definitely a change from the standard weekday fare of grits, eggs and juice. She looked determined today. He wondered why.

"I see you've decided to join the land of the living," she greeted him.

"What are you talking about? It's 6:30." Mal checked his watch. It wasn't 6:30. "Ohmigod! It's 7:45. I'm so late."

"Calm down, Mal. I called Gina. She's got it covered. Besides, I need you today."

"What the devil is going on here? How could I oversleep? Did you mess with the alarm, Ray?"

"A little, yes. Listen to me, Mal. We need to talk. The business can wait."

Rachel rarely went to such lengths, so he calmly sat and listened. She expressed her opinions about the direction of the new store. Usually a silent partner, Rachel found her voice. They spent the morning at the table discussing the state of the business. Ultimately, they concluded that more promotion was needed and that the new location would be successful—but it would take focus and effort to improve it to the level of the first store.

Mal turned the main store over to his capable store manager, Gina. J&J became his focus. He hired a freelance PR rep to help plan a new launch. It required hundreds of hours of planning and production, but it eventually worked. A smart commercial was crafted. The store became an important part of the local landscape and began to turn a profit.

Mal realized that the problem with his second venture had less to do with obsession and more to do with focusing his passion and efforts.

Wisdom to Take Away

- The first-hit principle suggests that there is a time warp in the ultimate achievement of entrepreneurial success. In other words, success usually does not come overnight. This principle works in conjunction with the bucket principle, which suggests that the time warp of success carries with it an opportunity or "bucket" with a cumulative requirement that must be met.

- You as an entrepreneur have a "bucket" that you must fill to overflowing before you will see any significant returns from your investment or labor. Fill your bucket with the same things that make up the investment curve—time, talent, and treasure. Your only actions will be to add to or take from the bucket.

- Unfortunately in America, some entrepreneurs are saddled with oversized buckets because of color, gender, socioeconomic status, or age. Consequently, an African American woman from the housing projects who may be of senior age has a gigantic barrel to fill, while a white male from upper-middle-class roots who has just finished his MBA may have a teacup to fill.

- There is a silver lining: Although some may have larger buckets to fill than others, the reality is that you can never get more out of your bucket than you put in. Therefore, even though the African American woman is forced to spend more time filling her bucket, if she can stay in the race and endure to the end, her rewards will flow like a mighty stream. People will be amazed at her performance, though they may have difficulty understanding the obstacles she had to overcome and the power she gained by being able to persevere.

WEEK

16

The Principle of
Increasing Returns

Securing the Future

Brian Mitchell, a former police officer, could pinpoint the exact time of his business breakthrough. Barely a year after starting his consulting firm, he had won the contract of his dreams. Mitchell Security Specialists (he labored for months on the name) had turned a nice profit in its opening months because of low overhead and few employees. But the business had experienced no major growth—until Dolefield.

The Dolefield House, which had a century-old reputation for hosting exclusive parties attended by diplomats, dignitaries, and statesmen, wanted his services. Winning this contract to provide the daily security for the building was money in the bank. It would propel his business to a new level.

The next months were like a dream. He had regular work for his full-time employees and was able to hire additional part-timers for events security. Business thrived, and he diversified, opening a side business providing private security for celebrities. He seemed to have the Midas touch.

Only later did he realize his success was a result of hard work and lifelong experience.

How could he forget the late hours in the office, the difficult choices, the stiff competition, not to mention the endless outflow of money just to get the company started. He'd spent twenty-five years on the police force gaining knowledge and making contacts. The breakthrough Dolefield contract may have happened overnight, but he had spent a lifetime gathering resources to get him to that point.

Wisdom to Take Away

- Any course on business theory or business economics will include a review of the law of diminishing returns. This law states that committing resources to a process to achieve a business objective will typically produce gains up to a point. At some point the gains will peak, and thereafter, regardless of how many more resources are added to the process, the gain will decrease and continue diminishing over time.
- The principle of increasing returns states that for minority and female entrepreneurs, there is a diametrically opposite phenomenon: Their efforts typically will produce little gain for the system until they reach breakthrough, or the first-hit mark. Beyond this first hit, all their efforts produce significant gain that is cumulative and allows the return curve to grow exponentially.
- The power of this principle is that once you are engaged in an entrepreneurial venture, smaller quantities of effort on your part will start to yield significant gains in your business. At this point, your business starts to experience explosive growth.

;

The RAF vs.
RFA Principle

The Bombardier

Buck Brown walked briskly toward the elevator, eager to reach his fifth-floor office. His sure step and crisp stride were evidence of his military training. Buck knew the last mail of the day had arrived. He was hoping to receive notification of an award of a large government contract. David Choe, the contracts administrator of the agency that was letting the contract, had committed to sending out all notifications to bidders by noon today. All day Buck had envisioned the award letter sitting on his desk. He had a good feeling about this particular procurement and looked forward to a positive response.

As he waited for the gray steel doors to open, Buck did a mental inventory of the hard work he had put into preparing the proposal. He had thoroughly researched the construction site to uncover any hidden issues. He had spent weeks studying the scope of the job and had targeted his bid to address all issues.

As the elevator approached his floor, Buck could feel tiny droplets of sweat forming on his temples. His once crisp collar felt moist as the doors finally opened.

Buck hurried past his receptionist, Tonya, who was busy on the phone with a client in need of a fax. Buck didn't have time for pleasantries at the moment anyway. He rushed into his office and quickly closed the door behind him. The large orange envelope lay on his desk. The flimsy enclosure forewarned of an unfavorable outcome. He doubted that the thick contract that usually accompanied a positive notification could be condensed to the one or two pages the orange envelope appeared to contain.

Sitting down, Buck read the heartbreaking words informing him that the contract was being awarded to a competitor. With the letter still clutched in his hands, Buck closed his eyes and sank deep into his chair. "I missed it. I missed it." The words rang in his head, although his lips were still.

Buck's thoughts raced back to another time in his life. He was no longer a businessman seated in his smooth leather office chair but was a bombardier crouched in an airplane high over enemy territory. At his side, just within arm's reach, were mountains of maps, computer printouts, jet-stream velocity projections, and colorful images generated from the Air Force's high-powered geographical information system. He had critical data on wind speeds, elevations, ambient temperatures and pressures, and the speed of the plane as it headed to its destination. He made calculations from the data, then dropped his payload.

After a few moments that to Buck seemed an eternity, he heard through his headphone that he had missed the target. Buck knew the next step. Either the plane would come around again for a second shot at the target, or the captain would cut his losses and return to base. Through his bomb-sight, Buck could see a faint cloud of dust rising from a smoldering building that lay in ruins on the ground below. Nearby, the enemy's flag still waved over the munitions factory that was the target of the crew's bombing mission.

Buck and his crew members were expressing frustration about missing the target, when they heard the calm, controlled voice of the captain. "Settle in, fellas. We're coming around again for a second try. Buck, I need you to look at the feedback from the first shot, adjust your parameters, and get prepared to drop the reserve payload."

"Aye aye, sir," Buck replied with a sense of relief that he would get a second chance to redeem himself and improve his aim.

Buck reached down within the cramped quarters of the bombardier's chamber, grabbed a handful of papers, and confidently calculated a new set of coordinates for the next run. As the plane came around for one last attempt to destroy the factory, the captain spoke through the plane's sound system. "Okay, Buck, we're now in range of the target. You are free to release your load when you're ready."

"Aye aye, sir," Buck replied as he checked his coordinates one last time and dropped the remaining bombs on the target.

Opening his eyes, Buck was back in his office. His heart was still racing from his momentary journey back to his days as a bombardier during the war. He stood, the now moist letter still curled in his fingers, and walked to the window. As the warm sun touched his face, he remembered the lesson he'd learned during the war. Buck whispered to himself confidently, "Its okay. I'll just take a new aim, adjust my coordinates, and try again."

Wisdom to Take Away

- A military bombardier uses multiple pieces of information to make calculations before he drops his bombs. Rarely does he score a bulls-eye on the first attempt. After dropping the first bombs, the bombardier quickly assesses how close he came to the target, adjusts his coordinates, and prepares for another try.
- Successful entrepreneurs are also required to make multiple attempts at hitting their business targets.

Unfortunately, many business people follow the technique of RAF (ready, aim, fire) in reaching their business objectives. Too often they are proficient at executing the ready and aim steps but never get around to firing (taking action or pulling the trigger).

- Successful entrepreneurs are adept at utilizing the technique of RFA (ready, fire, aim). They prepare to fire, they pull the trigger and aggressively integrate feedback from these actions in order to adjust the aim, and fire again. They tend to fire in rapid bursts as they quickly move closer and closer to hitting their intended targets.

18

The Steps Versus Elevator Principle

Conditioned for the Long Haul

Upon returning from the Korean War in 1954, Buddy Lowell set his sights on getting a job. He looked for several weeks before he finally met Mr. Miller, who took enough interest in Buddy to ask what type of experience he had. Since Buddy's sparse background included only farming and army, he didn't have much to offer in the way of skills. After reviewing Buddy's credentials, Mr. Miller said he couldn't hire him.

"If somebody doesn't give me a job, I'll never gain any experience," Buddy exclaimed, feeling he had nothing to lose.

Moved by Buddy's strong desire to work, Mr. Miller decided to give Buddy a chance. He offered him a job driving a truck delivering toys. The job paid a starting salary of $22 a week, a decent salary in the rural South at the time.

Buddy had no intention of being a truck driver forever. He enrolled in a two-year program at the local community college and attended professional development programs at Georgia Tech, the Tuck School at Dartmouth College, and various local educational institutions. Within a year, he landed a better-paying job at the post office. But with a growing family, he needed to find more work. So, in addition to his day job, Buddy took a part-time job as a night janitor.

Because Buddy exhibited strong leadership skills in his cleaning job, he was asked to lead a crew of janitorial workers. One night one of the best workers on his crew was fired because he accidentally broke an ashtray. Upset that the man was unjustly fired, Buddy quit. Within a week he had found a job at another cleaning service that paid more money and gave him more responsibility. Buddy quickly became the manager for a crew of nine people.

Realizing the profit margins in the janitorial-services business, Buddy took the next step and bought his way into the business. Luckily, his boss decided he wanted to retire and agreed to sell Buddy stock in the company. His initial stock purchase gave him approximately 33 percent of the company. As the business began to prosper, Buddy left his post office job to run the janitorial business full-time. Even though he had limited cash, the owner agreed to let Buddy continue to buy equity in the firm using his current and future earnings as collateral.

Under Buddy's ownership the company grew rapidly. He discovered that many customers wanted to purchase the cleaning products he used, so he started a second business that focused on sales of cleaning supplies. His commitment to excellence made it possible for Buddy to increase his customer base through word-of-mouth and marketing.

From the very beginning, Buddy was confident that he could make the business a success. He recognized the importance of not growing too fast. He knew that incremental growth was better for his business and certainly safer. He knew to be patient with existing and potential customers and often postponed new cleaning projects until he had mastered the ones that he already had. Maintaining steady, incremental, and controllable growth minimized his risks and served Buddy well.

Wisdom to Take Away

- Many small business owners possess an "elevator mentality" as it pertains to entrepreneurial success and business growth. Like a person who steps into an elevator, pushes a button, and is immediately whisked to the floor of their choosing, they believe that success can be produced with similar effort.
- Others, like Buddy, prefer the incremental approach of taking small, calculated steps that move them toward a worthy goal. They believe in the value of taking the time to build a foundation before climbing to the next level.

Taking Incremental Steps

1. Forces you to condition yourself for the long haul, to hone your skills, and then to steadily improve upon them.
2. Allows you to adjust to the ever-changing and variable conditions of the journey. As you collect more data—and make mistakes—you'll be moving slowly enough to adjust before a mistake can become fatal.
3. Gives you the opportunity to build an infrastructure, which will support your ultimate success. It does no good to achieve high levels of success only to find that you're unable to handle the demands that success brings.
4. Builds your confidence in your ability to overcome obstacles and to achieve. The more you achieve, the more confident you will become.

WEEK

19

The Invisible
Sixth Man Principle

Celtic Magic

Many sports teams have had successful championship runs. But few have achieved the level of long-term success obtained by the Boston Celtics. During the 1980s the team was one of the most successful franchises in the history of professional basketball. There were no last-minute struggles to win. The 1980s Celtics embodied the principle of the "sixth man." NBA teams can only field five players at a time; the sixth man is a key position because this player must be able to substitute for any of the starting players. The concept of the sixth man represents the concerted effort of the team. Consistently, the Celtics defeated opponents that statistically were far superior.

The Celtics were so successful because their members played well together and also played as a team; they had a remarkable rapport. The "no look" pass became a team signature. Rebounds, shots, assists—the Celtics could do it all. They seemed to be of one mind and body when on the court. Through this, they became more than the sum of their parts. They had in their ranks the invisible sixth man.

Wisdom to Take Away

- Experience has shown that successful entrepreneurs cannot and do not accomplish any great entrepreneurial feat alone. They must become proficient at team building and convincing others to work with them and for them. Entrepreneurs sometimes tend to build a team based solely on the technical skills (e.g., accounting, engineering, marketing) that an individual can bring to the team or on the individual's credentials. Technical skills and credentials are necessary and important, but there are other factors that are just as important.
- Qualities such as teamwork, loyalty, values congruence, and commitment to the company's vision will often energize the team to become more than the sum of its various parts. This sum is the sixth-man principle in action. Everything else being equal, these intangible qualities are the tiebreakers that determine if a company will become a consistent, dependable, long-term winner.

WEEK
20

The Principle of Opposites

The Odd Couple

Lenora Wilkins was a true leader. In high school, she had led the debate team and the student council and was a peer leader in her circle of friends. She had an uncanny ability to make wise decisions and to choose the right friends.

Jill was her confidante and staunch, true friend; LaVerne, her cousin, acted as social activities planner. Her husband Randolph, her best friend, was a jester at heart. His humor made her say yes to his marriage proposal. Theresa, Jack, and Hunter were college friends who had kept in touch. Lenora was the center of the support system. Her gift for making teams work eventually yielded a small consulting firm that was fast becoming a success in the field of computer networking within its first five years.

One particular contract tested both Lenora's ability to judge character and to manage her staff. Jill and Theresa were top consultants for her; Lenora didn't have enough qualified personnel that she trusted to meet the contract requirements. Hunter, usually her ace, was out of town with his family. She faced a difficult decision—there were two key spots and four qualified associates to choose from.

The job would be prestigious—a feather in the cap of whomever was chosen—and everyone knew it. Each wanted a spot on the team.

Lenora pondered in private as she doodled pictures in the margin of a legal pad. Each picture represented one of the candidates.

First, she scribbled Darron Singleton, her newest employee. He had already earned a reputation among his colleagues for his thoroughness. She drew him with a large head, which made her laugh since that image was so fitting of his personality. Next, she drew Lisa Johnson, long-haired with huge curls and a big smile. Lisa was a longtime employee who handled projects well. The only possible drawback was Lisa's occasional tardiness. Lenora's next depiction was Oliver Nichols, a trusted employee, though not yet as talented as some of his colleagues. Oliver was also a team player, an asset to the cause. Finally, there was Rose Johns, a bit of a loner but indisputably the most talented of her consulting team. Rose was task-driven and hardworking. But she lacked social finesse.

Lenora began the final deliberations on the team and emerged from her office confident about her choices. She had learned long ago not to second-guess herself.

The staff positioned themselves around her outer office to find out who had made it aboard. Lenora hesitated a few seconds, then adjusted her focus to the announcement.

"First, let me say that we will have other projects for each of you to participate in. So I don't want anyone to feel that being involved here is crucial to your success at the firm." She was trying to be direct, not to hedge the truth.

Four pairs of eyes fixed on her as she finished. "I've chosen Oliver and Rose. That may come as a bit of a surprise to some of you, but I made this decision based on the objectives of the team. Oliver knows best how to cooperate and manage the relationship between our client and us, and Rose will maintain focus on the task and timetables stipulated. They may appear opposites, but I'm confident. Congratulations!"

With that Oliver and Rose nearly embraced—saved only by mutual discomfort. Lenora chuckled at the future the two would have. She had chosen the two with opposite talents because they would best complement one another to form a team.

Wisdom to Take Away

- An accepted principle in the field of magnetism is that opposite poles attract and similar poles repel each another. The poles are controlled by magnetic attraction. These rules of magnetism can also apply in determining how entrepreneurs build their teams.
- The principle of opposites suggests that entrepreneurs building a team must be careful not to look for people like them but instead must actively seek those who will offer diverse talents.
- A team that is diverse in ideas, background, technical skills, ethnicity, gender, geographical origins, and experience prepares the entrepreneur for handling a myriad of situations and business challenges. More important, a diverse team is one that will be more competitive.

21

The Principle of Trustworthiness

A Big Bite

LaDina Henry felt doomed. With only six days left to complete decorating a client's guest house, she worried herself silly. Decorating was a passion she had developed since having her first Barbie house. At age six, she took it upon herself to make pillows for the furniture and to add color to the walls. She was a born decorator—or so her mother always reminded her. Throughout her teens, she pursued only artistic endeavors. Instead of college, she apprenticed with a local design firm to cut her teeth in the business.

Now LaDina was making a splash. Her last job went off without a hitch. The clients, Mr. and Mrs. Newman, were in line with her vision. They seemed to love everything she did. That's why they had hired her again to redecorate the guest house. They were having family in for the holidays but did not have time themselves to make the space cozier. LaDina seemed to be a perfect fit. Yet, she'd never done an entire house before, especially one with five bedrooms.

Henry Designs lacked the staff for such a job, but LaDina let her pride and the potential payoff get the better of her. Before carefully reviewing her schedule, she leaped at the chance to work with the Newmans again. Not only did they appreciate her work, but they also could send referrals her way, as their social set redecorated the way most people change their clothes. She hired a few temp employees to help with the finishing touches and relied mostly on her two assistants to back her on major decisions.

Still, there would not be enough time to complete the last two bedrooms and baths. Everyone was already putting in ten hours a day. She couldn't ask for or afford more than that. Either she would have to work additional hours herself, which would take her away from planning upcoming project schedules and meeting with clients, or she would have to risk other business to save this project.

LaDina knew she had to do something. She opted for honesty.

She called Mrs. Newman to ask for an extension. To her surprise, Mrs. Newman was quite understanding, but Mr. Newman viewed it as incompetence on her part. LaDina tried reducing her original price to appease him, but he rebuffed her. She lost the repeat business, but she gained a valuable lesson about undertaking more than she could manage.

Wisdom to Take Away

- Trust is one of the most important qualities in business. In other words, entrepreneurs must be worthy of someone's confidence and trust.
- Many theories exist about how to build trust and confidence, but there are some common themes that an entrepreneur would be wise to remember:

  1. Stay in touch with your skill set.
  2. Do not oversell yourself. It is better to undersell yourself and then exceed the customer's expectations.

3. Manage the customer's expectations. Constantly assure that what the customer is expecting and what you are delivering are the same. The customer's expectations can be managed by maintaining frequent and open communications.
4. Deliver. Do what you say you're going to do, consistently.
5. Never, never lie to the customer. Lies always come back to haunt you.

22

The "No True Meritocracy" Principle

Eggs in a Basket

Donna LeRoi wanted to be an Internet entrepreneur. Hailing from Shreveport, Louisiana, with all the spice of Cajun cooking and the mystery of Rampart Street, she accepted the first job she was offered upon relocating to Cleveland, Ohio. Unfortunately, she found herself stuck in a traffic jam at a local advertising agency, surrounded by unmoving bureaucrats and stubborn regulations.

She was acutely aware that movers and shakers in Cleveland were independent of the corporate schematic, and she had tried twice in the past six months to reorganize her Web site into a revenue-producing business while maintaining her 9-to-5 job. She had drive, but still it took her considerable time to upgrade her Web page, add graphics, and plan a simple marketing strategy. After months of hard work, she had a site dedicated to helping businesses upgrade their sites using the new Flash technology. It yielded an impressive number of hits each day. She had technical and creative talent, and she had uncovered a niche that was ideal for the Web world.

She was growing restless with her day job and needed to find a way to take her business to the next level. The money was beginning to flow in, and the site was popular and engaging, but she felt she lacked true recognition for her accomplishments. Success would be more satisfying, she reasoned, if she could get the press interested in her site—perhaps by winning a few Web site awards. She set out to make this goal a reality by filling out award applications.

Weeks later, Donna received an invitation to meet the judges at the informal luncheon for an award presented by Cyber Designs. She was a semifinalist for a major award that included a $10,000 prize. She was overjoyed and quit her advertising job in anticipation of instant recognition and the financial award.

She somehow felt she couldn't lose. Her quick success, to this point, made her overconfident and willing to put all of her eggs in one basket. After all, hits on her site were growing every month. And a quick study of her competition led her to believe that she must be the front-runner. Her handful of competitors were newer to Web business, and their sites were less interactive and not as richly designed.

At the luncheon, the Cyber Designs judges, one woman and three men, stood stone-faced at the door. Nothing in their eyes gave a hint one way or the other. Mr. Comstock, the head judge, approached her cautiously. "Are you Ms. LeRoi?"

"Why, yes I am. I hope you enjoyed my site," she said reaching to shake his hand. Embarrassed, he took her hand just long enough to meet the social obligation. It was the weakest hand shake that she had felt since leaving the South.

Comstock looked away before her eyes could meet his. After a brief, curt conversation, he left her to focus on the other contestants. Donna found his manner unsettlingly familiar; she'd met people like this before in many situations, and the feeling left her cold. Although she didn't have proof, she had the distinct impression that Comstock did not like her because of her race or gender—perhaps both. But she looked around and noticed another white woman semifinalist who received a much warmer response from Mr. Comstock.

In that instant, she felt certain he was racially biased. Her tan skin turned beet red. She was furious that racism could permeate what she believed was the color-blind world of the Internet. Donna sensed the award was not going to be hers. She was right; a white male won. His site was months behind hers in traffic and technology.

Donna learned a valuable lesson about business. She learned that effort alone is a personal reward and that merit is wholly subjective. And she learned that although America is a democracy, it is not a true meritocracy.

Wisdom to Take Away

- Many Americans believe that our country is a true meritocracy—that the best and brightest always rise to the top and earn their just reward. This view fails to take into consideration the effects of racism, sexism, and classism. These "isms" act as brakes, slowing down the recognition and rewards that should be realized by talented minority and female entrepreneurs.
- If you are a person of color or a woman, you no doubt understand and appreciate that America is not yet a true meritocracy. We have no true system whereby the talented are chosen and moved ahead solely on the basis of achievement. Leaders are not always elected or appointed on the basis of abstract intellectual criteria. The meritocracy principle dictates that minority and female entrepreneurs must work twice as hard and become twice as intellectually agile as

their counterparts in order to realize the fruits of their labor.

- By working to be twice as good, entrepreneurs will accelerate the time frame required for them to receive their just reward and position themselves for even more exciting entrepreneurial opportunities.

The Principle of Diminished Expectations

Heads Up, Avon

The year is 1978. In the midst of the quiet desperation of the 1970s, a joyful noise can be heard. In a tiny downtown office, located above a popular delicatessen in Tampa, Florida, Avon is celebrating with his two partners.

"Hallelujah Jesus! I never thought I'd see the day when minorities would get a fair chance in government contracting."

Avon had just received a call from one of his friends who was a lobbyist in the state legislature.

"Avon," she announced over the phone, "I wanted to inform you that not only has the city council passed groundbreaking legislation supporting minority- and female-owned businesses, but the state has also passed legislation requiring state agencies to diversify their supplier pool and open up more contract opportunities for minority- and female-owned businesses."

Avon, who had earned his undergraduate degree in architecture from Howard University, had personally lobbied for the passage of this economic development legislation and was elated by the new business possibilities that could result.

Like many of his peers, Avon had grown frustrated and angry. Whenever he attended the prebid conferences, he saw the same people from the same companies with the same smug grins on their faces. Avon had grown to despise those grins; they often revealed an untold story about the inevitable outcome of the bidding process. Avon often remembered lingering after the formal meeting and over-hearing conversations between government officials and company representatives about some golf outing they had last year. They even knew each other's families and often vacationed together. How, Avon wondered, could he ever compete with this "old boy" network?

"Without these minority business programs, man, we wouldn't have a chance. With the new legislation, we may have a shot!" Avon said to his partners as they packed up to close shop for the day.

"The proof is in the pudding," replied Walter. "We'll start putting this new attitude to the test starting tomorrow."

Putting the government's new programs to the test was exactly what Avon and his crew started to do. They began by researching which government agencies had the greatest need for the services Avon's firm provided. Most depart-ments used some form of architectural and engineering design services, but Avon wisely chose to focus on the state's transportation and public works departments. He knew from his research that these departments had the largest capital budgets and showed the greatest promise for business opportunities.

As Avon and his team focused their marketing efforts, they were successful at scheduling and meeting with the department administrators. In retrospect, they concluded that their status as one of a few minority-owned architec-tural and engineering firms in the area may have made the firm more visible. But at the time, they didn't analyze the reason; they were just happy to have the opportunity to meet key government decisionmakers.

One agency they met with in the next six months showed special promise. The state transit administration had just been awarded a major transportation grant to help develop and expand the state's high-speed rail system. The project would require significant architectural and engineering services. Also, the agency was headed by a Hispanic woman, Ms. Cortez, which gave Avon and his team some hope that they might be considered for a piece of this emerging business.

Avon's instincts were correct. Shortly after meeting with Ms. Cortez, he received a welcome call from the purchasing office.

"Mr. Bellamy, we have reviewed the qualifications of your firm and feel that you might be in a position to provide some key technical services to us as we expand our high-speed rail infrastructure. We would like you to conduct a site survey for some planned expansions we have on the books. So that we can get this approved quickly, we'll have to keep the contract below ten thousand dollars per transaction. This way we can dramatically shorten the approval process and put your firm to work right away. Are you interested?"

Stunned by the mixed events unfolding before him, Avon paused to gather his thoughts. Ten thousand dollars was a very small contract, but this could be a good opportunity to gain a foothold for future projects.

"Mr. Bellamy, are you still there?" the procurement officer asked.

"Yes, yes, I'm interested. You need the cost of the labor to be less than ten thousand dollars. I'm sure we can work around that. What's the next step?" Avon responded.

"Please meet with me next week. We will have all the paperwork ready for you to sign. Afterward your people can begin work immediately."

Before the phone was out of Avon's hand, Walter, who had overheard the conversation, was jumping all over him. "I don't believe what I just heard you agree to. Tell me if I'm wrong, but did you just agree to contract our services out for a mere ten thousand dollars?"

"Yes, I did." Avon defensively replied, as he looked out the window.

"With an agency that is going to be spending over one billion dollars, you mean to tell me that the best they can do is give us ten thousand dollars worth of business? Forget it! That won't even cover our overhead. I'm tired of this. They always want to give us the crumbs, while the white guys walk away with the loaf of bread. My vote is that we not accept this job."

Avon continued staring at the rush-hour traffic. "It's too late, Walter. I've made a commitment. Besides, the way I look at it, this is our golden opportunity to get our foot in the door. They can see how good we are up close."

Walter's angry retort came quickly. "Avon, for all these years, I've heard that we're too small and that we need to get bigger before they will trust us with large contracts. How will we ever get bigger if we keep accepting little contracts like this? Even though I disagree with this decision, I will support it." Walter stormed out of Avon's office and through the stairwell door.

Avon sat in his office, still staring out the window and repeating to himself, "Walter is right. Walter is right."

Uncertain about the outcome but even more determined to prove his firm's capabilities, Avon set out to execute the new contract with the transit administration. Focusing the effort of his best architects and engineers, Avon personally made sure that this customer would be taken care of very well. He had been working on the contract for only three weeks before he was hit with a bombshell.

"Hi ya, Avon! Long time no see." Laura smiled as she saw Avon walking out of the transit administration's drawing office. Laura Von Kueller was a transportation engineer who had worked with Avon at a previous job. Avon had left the company to start his own firm, and Laura had left about the same time to take a job with the state transit administration. Laura admired Avon and respected his intelligence and technical skills.

"Hello, Laura. What a pleasure to see you after all these years. I hear you're doing very well. How's your husband?" The conversation would probably be reduced to pleasantries, he surmised.

"He's well, thank you. I heard that your firm was working on the new contract, and I wanted to give you a heads up on some things you should know about. Do you mind if I speak to you off the record?"

"You know you can, Laura. You and I go way back." Avon chuckled.

"Seriously, Avon. There's a lot happening on the project right now and . . . ." She hesitated, then restarted. "To make a long story short, the project manager that you're working for is a real jerk. He's always talking about how he has tried using minority- and women-owned businesses on projects in the past but that they never seem to work up to his standards. He thinks you're a nice guy, but he doesn't have high expectations for the work your guys are doing. He thinks that you're here as some kind of affirmative-action experiment and that once you've completed your little project you'll be out the door. I'm telling you this because I want you to watch your back. I'm headed to a meeting across town, but make sure you call me if you need anything."

Stunned by this disturbing news, Avon hugged Laura. "Thanks for the heads up, Laura."

Avon arrived at work early the next Monday morning. He called an impromptu staff meeting and explained his conversation with Laura Von Kueller. "It is my understanding that, for some reason, the project manager we work for may not have high expectations for the quality and thoroughness of our work. I don't know if his expectations are based upon the fact that we are minority-owned or not. In the final analysis, I don't care what's behind his reaction. I just wanted to reiterate to you my expectations that we not just meet but surpass our high level of accuracy, precision, attention to detail, and thoroughness on this job. If we meet our own personal and professional standards on this project, we'll be successful. I appreciate the effort you've made so far and ask you to keep up the good work."

And so without incident Avon's team kept up the good work. Inspired and motivated by the reality under which they were working, they proceeded to complete, in a timely fashion, a professional and thorough site survey. Avon's firm did so well that Ms. Cortez and the project manager, Jack Delaney, wrote commendation letters for Avon's firm. The reputation of Avon's firm was further enhanced when the agency selected the engineering model developed by Avon's staff as the basis for all future site surveys.

Twenty years have passed and Avon and his partners are still in business. Blateck, Inc. has grown significantly from a staff of ten to more than fifteen hundred employees. It no longer focuses only on state and local government opportunities but has expanded its operation worldwide, with offices all over the United States and in London, West Africa, Brazil, and the Caribbean.

Avon and Walter study the New York City skyline from their twenty-fourth-floor offices in the World Trade Center. Both men are about thirty pounds heavier than two decades earlier and have less hair, but they are very happy about the company they've built.

Walter breaks the silence. "You know, Avon, if you hadn't made the decision to take that ten-thousand-dollar job twenty years ago, we wouldn't be where we are today. Man, I remember after we blew them away on that job how they wanted us to do more work for them and at much higher labor rates! Even better, once our reputation was established, suddenly the larger firms wanted us to be on their team for the multi-billion-dollar contracts. Thank goodness we've won our fair share of them."

Avon and Walter learned that no matter what the customer's expectations are, always exceed them. It helps if the customer has low or diminished expectations, because that makes it easier to exceed them.

Both men chuckle as they gather their laptops and prepare for a trip to South America. As they walk toward the elevator, they think about how they will exceed the expectations of their new South American clients.

Wisdom to Take Away

- The term "glass ceiling" is often used to describe the resistance to advancement that minority and female executives experience as they work to advance in an organization. The world of entrepreneurship has a "concrete ceiling." I use the image of concrete because, unlike glass, concrete offers no chance to see what could be achieved. This resistance is often in the form of diminished expectations. Some decision makers, unfortunately, still have a preconceived view that businesses owned and operated by blacks, Hispanics, Asians, and women are not of the same quality and do not have equal capabilities as firms owned and operated by white males.
- The key to benefiting from the principle of diminished expectations when you're faced with this situation is to focus your resources on dramatically exceeding the expectations of your client. If your client insists on lowering the bar, you'll find it that much easier to far exceed the expectations and score points for your firm.

The Principle of
the White Angel

It's Not What You Know
but Whom You Know

On a humid Monday morning in downtown Washington, D.C., the dark and threatening skies reflected Eloise's mood. "I'm sick and tired of established firms getting all the business, while we start-up entrepreneurs continue to get the crumbs," Eloise said to herself. "They keep telling us that we're competing on a level playing field, but I always feel I'm climbing Mount Everest," she sadly mused.

Eloise was frustrated. She was raised by hardworking parents who taught her that if she worked hard, studied hard, and excelled at her profession, she too could begin to live the American dream. Despite the harsh reality in the Mississippi delta region, where Eloise's family lived, her parents had painstakingly planted the belief in their twelve children that even with the perceived hypocrisy of white America, the ideals upon which America was built did provide opportunity for smart and intelligent people to prosper. Eloise took her parents at their word and dedicated herself to excelling in school. She left the delta swamps and earned her degree in marketing and public relations from the Wharton School of Business at the University of Pennsylvania.

Determined to become a successful entrepreneur, Eloise leveraged her degree and began pursuing short-term corporate jobs, fully intending to use them to gain valuable experience and hone her technical skills until she was ready to set out on her own. Seven years into her career, she left a well-paying Madison Avenue job to start her own marketing and public relations consulting firm.

But she found the American dream turning into a nightmare. Eloise had used all of her savings to capitalize her business, and she saw her financial base crumbling before her eyes as she struggled to win billable consulting contracts. Although she had excellent skills, she found that the marketing and public relations business was a closed shop if you happened to be a black female. After repeated rejections, it dawned on her that the industry was dominated by the "good old boy" network. No matter how gifted she was, no matter how professional her proposals were, no matter that her price was 10–15 percent cheaper than her competition's, Eloise came to the sad realization that the playing field was not level for her.

Depressed, discouraged, and nearly broke, Eloise decided to call it quits. She phoned her former boss, Bob. She thought, "I'll ask him for my old job back. He always appreciated my work." Eloise and Bob had established a warm and supportive working relationship, and he had been one of the main people cheering Eloise on to step out and take her chances as an entrepreneur.

"I must admit, Eloise, I'm surprised and disappointed that things didn't work out better for you. What happened?" Bob said when the two met for lunch.

"Well, I really felt that business was a meritocracy and that the best and brightest always get ahead. But I was wrong," she said dejectedly. "It's just not possible for me to succeed in this white-male-dominated industry. Most of my potential customers won't even return my phone calls."

Bob smiled and whispered to Eloise, "I guess there are some things that Wharton just didn't teach you."

The comment surprised her. "What do you mean by that?"

"Eloise, it's like this. I am a white male businessperson. I've been one all of my life. Although I have great disdain for the old boy network, I understand that it is real, it is powerful, and it is difficult to break into."

Eloise was somewhat shocked but appreciative that Bob felt comfortable enough to share his thoughts with her. He continued.

"Eloise, the key to breaking into business is to find someone to sponsor you into that network."

"But Bob, the old boy network is made up of, well, old white men. Who would want to sponsor me?"

Bob laughed. "Hey, we're not all bad guys, you know. There are some good white males around."

"Bob, you know that I didn't mean it that way. It's just that I've had so many doors closed in my face—I'm a little skeptical."

"Yes, yes I understand," Bob replied. "You know, Eloise, it's like finding yourself an angel, someone who is already in the network and who is open and forthright enough to sponsor you."

"Go on."

The conversation between Bob and Eloise did go on, long into the afternoon. As they had their last cup of coffee, Bob leaned forward, looked Eloise straight in the eye, and in a very serious tone said, "Here's what I'll do for you. I have an old classmate I'd like to introduce you to. He's in need of a marketing and public relations consultant to help him position his new Internet business. Here's his phone number. Wait until Thursday to call him so that I can grease the skids for you."

Eloise thanked Bob for his support. During her cab ride home she realized how much she missed their talks.

Eloise waited until Thursday and then called Bob's friend. George's voice was pleasant and surprisingly accommodating. "Yes, Eloise, I've heard all about you and the good work you do. Your timing is impeccable. We're about to take our company public, and I was looking for a consulting firm just like yours to help position us for the offering. You'll be working with our chief financial officer, Lynnette Young. She's expecting a call from you so that the two of you can work out the terms and conditions of your contract."

Eloise was flabbergasted. In a matter of minutes, she had closed her first deal without even meeting the client. "Thank you, George. I appreciate the opportunity you're giving me, and I won't let you down. I'll call Ms. Young immediately."

Wisdom to Take Away

- Business in America is conducted through relationships. There are exceptions to this rule, but new entrepreneurs must learn to leverage relationships with established members of the business network they are trying to break into. Someone with an inside track will frequently sponsor a promising entrepreneur.
- Some say that "power is never given; it must be taken." Conversely, help can be given only when it is accepted. Learn to recognize when you need help. Be willing to ask for it, and more important, be willing to accept it. No one is a self-made success. We all benefit from the support of others throughout the ventures we take on in life.
- Minority and women entrepreneurs cannot and must not restrict themselves to doing business only with other minority and women business people. You must be proactive at building relationships with members of the white business community. A win-win business proposition exists for those brave enough to change and who challenge the status quo.

WEEK
25

The Focus on
What Matters Principle

Smoke and Mirrors

Derrick Williams was a former model. Everything he wore had a designer label. Even his socks were designer. He attributed the accounts he'd landed recently to his wardrobe and his wining and dining of clients. Derrick believed in selling the "look" that makes clients feel they're dealing with a winner.

One meeting changed his perspective on all his adornments. Derrick, who had just opened his own financial planning consulting firm, finally landed a lunch with Westin Smith, a wealthy annuities tycoon. Derrick sent Smith a prospectus of possible investment ventures. The proposal was rushed—not his best effort—but Derrick believed it would tell only half the story.

Derrick had heard that Smith was not easily impressed, so he pulled out all stops for his lunch presentation. First, he purchased a new suit, new shoes, and a new briefcase. Next, he made lunch reservations at a chic new restaurant whose prices were as famous as the cuisine. The decor was certain to impress, he thought. Finally, Derrick arranged for a limo to pick up Smith, even though his office was only four blocks away.

Verve, the restaurant, was decorated with high-end furnishings and paintings. Derrick rarely went to such places, since they were out of his price range. Sure, he had to have a few lunches and dinners at cutting-edge establishments to keep up appearances, but he never felt comfortable in them. Westin Smith arrived on schedule.

"Good afternoon, Mr. Smith. I've so been looking forward to meeting with you. Have a seat." Derrick was trying his best to please.

"No, thank you. I won't be staying." Smith looked deadly serious.

Derrick could barely breathe. He adjusted his designer tie. "Mr. Smith, I don't see how . . . "

"Williams, you are trying to impress me. That bothers me. Did you really believe a fancy restaurant would make up for the poor prospectus you gave me? You barely projected beyond the second quarter. What happens then?"

"Sir, I'm sorry if you feel that way. I only wanted to . . . "

Derrick knew he was in trouble. His defense was flimsy. He had skimped on business details to concentrate on making an impression, and it appeared he would pay for it. He already had: the lunch, the clothes, the limo. He could feel some cosmic accountant tallying the total bill.

"In fact, Williams, I don't think we have anything further to discuss."

With that, he disappeared as quickly as he had materialized. The waiter came to the table to take the order. "Good afternoon, sir. My name is Philip and I'll be your. . . "

Derrick couldn't hear him. The only words that registered were those of Westin Smith. Derrick had made a crucial mistake. He allowed himself to believe that appearance was more important than substance. He never made that mistake again.

Wisdom to Take Away

- Too often entrepreneurs focus on details that do not add value to the process of realizing business opportunities. They pay too much attention to the type of suit they wear, the type of briefcase they carry, the type of car they drive, and the type of neighborhood they live in, believing that these factors will determine their level of success or failure.
- Such items may have a bearing on someone's impression of you, but it is doubtful that they will dictate your level of success. Your time and resources are better spent focusing on matters that will add value to your entrepreneurial process.
- Value-added tasks might include spending more time on market research, hiring a number cruncher to help you hone financial projects, or investing in a quality color laser printer so that your proposals are cleaner and crisper. It could mean investing in a state-of-the-art phone and teleconferencing system that shows your clients and prospects that you are a professional, sizable, and well-run company with which they can confidently do business.

26

The Roach Principle

Going for the Gold

"What am I doing in this wretched place?" Frazier screamed at the four dirty walls in his rented flat in downtown Kumasi, a city northwest of the capital of Ghana. Frazier had come to Kumasi to meet with some potential business partners for his new e-commerce initiative. This was his fourth trip to Kumasi in less than six weeks. Each previous trip had frustrated Frazier because he was unable to work out the business deal to his satisfaction. Every time he and his potential Ghanaian partners seemed near closing the deal, an obstacle would surface. At first they couldn't agree on the split of equity, but soon the disagreements centered around who would be in charge of the new company's day-to-day direction. Frazier understood that the Ghanaians should have operational control, but he was uneasy about their understanding of the e-commerce industry and what it took to be successful in this new Internet age.

Frazier's resolve and patience were wearing thin. The cost of flying back and forth between New York and Ghana was beginning to add up with no clear return on investment in sight. As Frazier laid in his unmade bed, which felt like a pile of crumpled newspapers instead of a mattress, he gazed at the ceiling of his hotel room. As he searched the plaster to find an answer to his predicament, he caught the movement of a large brown roach.

The hotel was the most modern one Frazier could find in Kumasi, but it still had difficulty controlling its insect population—especially the roaches. As the unsightly roach made its way across the broad expanse of ceiling, Frazier thought of his childhood in the housing projects of the South Bronx.

Frazier remembered how his parents fought a never-ending war against the little brown invaders. In the projects, it was impossible for a household to eradicate the unwelcome, filthy creatures completely. Even if one household put down insecticide to kill the pests, some would survive and simply relocate to the next household unit until the effect of the insecticide subsided. The roaches that survived kept coming back. But Frazier noticed that each time they returned, they seemed bigger, stronger, more resistant to the insecticide, and much bolder than before.

According to Frazier's recollection, the roaches became so bold that instead of waiting for darkness before beginning their mission to find more food, these brave insects started coming out during the day. They especially seemed to enjoy presenting themselves whenever Frazier's parents had company or when Frazier and his brothers invited their girlfriends over to visit.

The more Frazier's parents sprayed insecticide, the stronger the roaches seemed to become, and the more committed they seemed to survival.

After years of attempting to end the roaches' reign, Frazier's parents capitulated and changed their strategy. Instead of trying to kill all of the bugs, they accepted the reality that they would have to share their home with their unwanted guests.

As he lay in the hotel bed, Frazier suddenly began to laugh. He laughed so hard that tears ran down his cheeks.

He laughed even harder as he drew the analogy between his experience in trying to open a business in Ghana to that of his parents' obsession with destroying the roaches in his home. "Those little devils just kept coming back again and again and again. No matter what, they never gave up. They just came back stronger and wiser. Hey, if it worked for them, maybe it can work for me too!"

Frazier jumped from his bed, put on his dark blue business suit, reviewed his business plan, and made his way out the door and across town to meet with his potential business partners one more time. By the time the door to his room slammed shut, the little roach that had triggered Frazier's renewed effort had successfully negotiated the full length of cracked ceiling and scampered behind the picture of the Ashanti Goldfields that hung precariously on the wall.

Wisdom to Take Away

- The bad news for minority and female entrepreneurs is that like the roaches, they are constantly under attack and must fight for their business lives every single day. Many will become casualties of these efforts to reduce their ranks, but the good news is that a critical mass will survive and become even stronger by going through this weeding-out process. The secret here is to survive the screening and become a member of the critical mass.
- As businesses and industries go through the natural process of survival of the fittest, the key to being a survivor is to know your business and the industry and to do what you do extremely well. Maintain a passion for success, and master your trade.

PART THREE

Principles of Entrepreneurship Maintenance

WEEK
27

The Hannibal Principle

We will either find a way or make one.

—Hannibal

Where Do We Go from Here?

My professor of business strategy at the Tuck School of Business at Dartmouth College, Dr. James Brian Quinn, often used military war-gaming as a means of studying the tactical aspects of developing effective entrepreneurial strategies. Dr. Quinn referred to the strategies used in World War I and World War II. Patton, MacArthur, and Eisenhower were but a few of the great military minds he praised for their military genius and their contributions to the annals of war-gaming. But in my mind, the man who trumped them all was Hannibal, "the great Carthaginian." His military tactics and strategies are still taught today at such institutions as West Point and the Naval Academy.

Hannibal, one of the most celebrated military minds in the history of the world, lived in the North African city of Carthage. Carthage, founded in 814 B.C., was intelligently situated on a small bay within a large natural harbor, which is now called the Bay of Tunis. The area surrounding the city was quite fertile, and the Carthaginians established elaborate agricultural systems to feed their growing population. As the city grew and prospered, it expanded north and west to form Megara, or the suburbs, covering an area of approximately 490 square miles with a population surpassing 700,000.

The growth and expansion of Carthage is often compared to that of the British empire during the eighteenth and nineteenth centuries. During this period the British government was forced to follow its traders and "entrepreneurs" into new and often hostile territories. In order to establish trade routes, the British military conquered potential trading partners and established commerce infrastructures that were compatible with those in Britain.

Likewise, Hannibal and the Carthaginians followed a pattern of expanding their trade through strategic force. They established a powerful army to control land-based trade routes and built a mighty navy to control the sea-lanes. During the attempt for control of commerce, the Carthaginians began confronting Rome. Their initiatives continued despite the existence of a treaty that barred Roman shipping from the western Mediterranean and established the area as a Carthaginian lake.

Animosities between Hannibal and the Romans mounted as the years passed and the two superpowers competed for territory and economic opportunities. Finally, Hannibal attacked and burned the small city of Saguntum, initiating the Second Punic War between Carthage and Rome.

Not one to shy away from conflict, Hannibal began considering which route would best lead his troops to Rome. He had already concluded that he wanted to fight in Rome instead of Africa. Hannibal would not make the same mistake he made in the First Punic War when he let Rome take the initiative and was forced on the defensive.

Faced with this challenge, Hannibal analyzed whether to launch his attack by sea or by land. He rationalized that since the Romans had 225 galleys to his 50 galleys, he would be at a disadvantage if he attacked from the sea. Not only would he have a smaller power base, but his navy also would be sea-ravaged from the lengthy sojourn to Rome. He concluded that his best chance for a surprise attack was to march his army across the land routes.

In 218 B.C., the 26-year-old Hannibal set out to attack Rome with an army consisting of 90,000 foot soldiers, 12,000 horses, and 37 elephants. The arduous journey to Rome over land was long—nearly a thousand miles—and beset with obstacles. Hannibal and his men would have to cross a major river—the Rhone—and a number of smaller ones. Also in his path were two formidable mountain ranges, the Pyrenees and the Alps.

Furthermore, Hannibal's route would take him through territories controlled by the Numidians (north Africans), the Moors (Arab and African mixture), the Iberians (Spanish and Portuguese mixture), the Celts (British, Scottish, Irish mixture), and the Gauls (French ancestry). A peaceful march through these areas would not be likely. Hannibal knew that if he had to fight each group, he would not have enough soldiers left to challenge the Romans once he arrived in Italy.

Exercising his military genius, Hannibal quickly trained and deployed ambassadors who fanned out ahead of his army to meet these potential partners and establish binding agreements that they would not attack his troops as they marched through their territory, and that some groups would even join Hannibal's march to attack the Romans.

Although Hannibal lost a significant portion of his army during the march, his ability to establish these covenants with people who at one time were his enemies greatly reduced the attrition of his large but dwindling forces. By the time Hannibal reached Rome, he had lost more than half his army, yet he was still able to wage war on the Roman empire for fifteen years.

Like Hannibal, minority American and female entrepreneurs must resist the tendency to focus on the size and enormity of obstacles they face. They must instead look for new ways and develop innovative strategies to outmaneuver and outsmart the forces in American society that seek to keep minority and female entrepreneurs in a powerless position. Hannibal's march to Rome provides several lessons.

Wisdom to Take Away

- Don't look at the bars but instead look beyond them. All of us have paradigms that dictate how we view our world and ourselves. Unfortunately, some of our paradigms have been built on inaccurate data and often become psychological bars that tend to incarcerate our minds and disrupt the creativity of our thinking. Some of the obvious bars we construct include racism, sexism, classism, physical attributes, perceived wrongs, past injustices, or lack of education, to name a few. Our tendency to focus on the bars serves only to empower them, thus diverting valuable human energy from more productive entrepreneurial tasks such as defining our market niche, developing a winning business plan, and identifying sources of capital for our ventures.

- Learn to expect great things from yourself and others. The starting point for any human achievement of value is your belief in and desire to achieve the object of your dream. You become what you think about. If you think that all is lost and that you cannot win, you will achieve what you focus on.

- Assume full responsibility for your economic well-being and prosperity. Whenever you disown a problem, you relinquish all power to solve it. No one in America has the desire or conviction to fix the economic problems of the minority community but its members. Although the economic quagmire they find themselves in today is not totally of their own doing, the solutions and dedication to resolving these perplexing issues must and will come only from within that community.

- Aggressively seek to build win-win relationships with other minority firms and with mainstream firms. Very few companies today can stand by themselves for long. Some experts predict that the successful companies of the new millennium will be those that develop strategic and mutually beneficial teaming relationships with other companies. Minority and women entrepreneurs must not limit themselves to teaming only with businesses of similar ethnicity and gender. They should instead follow a parallel track and develop partnerships with any groups that seek to achieve common goals. Above all, make sure that the relationship is a win-win one so that it becomes a lasting and rewarding experience for both parties.

As young minority and female entrepreneurs you have some difficult days ahead. If you continue to look at your situation the way Hannibal viewed his thousands of years ago, you too can uncover weaknesses in your opponent's armor, attack his vulnerable spots, leverage the element of surprise, and continue your march to capture new business.

The
Grand Canyon Principle

The Lessons Within the Wonder

One of the greatest wonders on earth is the Grand Canyon. It is a magnificent site to behold—a place carved out of the earth by mighty rivers. Scientists estimate that it was formed over millions of years. Those who venture into it quickly realize its enormity—217 miles long, 10 miles wide, and approximately 1 mile deep. The Grand Canyon principle illustrates three critical points about successful entrepreneurship.

Wisdom to Take Away

- Over time, water is stronger than rock. A steady and relentless stream of water will eventually wear away the strongest stone. Likewise, entrepreneurs who are confident of their mission and who persist and persevere, even through the most trying of times, will ultimately wear down all obstacles.
- When you're in the Grand Canyon, you may climb many smaller mountains and hills, but the fact

remains that you'll still be in a hole. Successful entrepreneurs must recognize that it is not enough to win the "little battles" in their journey to canvass the canyon or achieve their major goals in business. They must become proficient at scaling the smaller mountains as they keep in sight the larger and grander objective.

- You cannot jump over a canyon with a series of small bounds. When you leap you must make it count. An entrepreneur must take great care in planning and determining how to commit time and resources to achieve the objectives that really count.

The Principle of Maintaining Congruence of Business and Values

The Liquor Store

"Yo, Robbo! What's happening, man?" The tall dark man with short black curls framing his face yelled in a squeaky voice at Robert as he maneuvered his shiny new sports car into the trash-strewn parking lot of the shopping center. Robert knew derelicts frequented the trash cans in the rear of the parking lot, but he had never known any of them to be bold enough to confront someone. As the man made his way to the driver's side of the car, Robert was slow to recognize his childhood buddy Griff.

Robert and Griff had grown up together in this violence-prone and drug-infested neighborhood in the heart of Pittsburgh. Although they were poor, neither of them knew it as kids, because both sets of parents took great pains to shield them from the harshness of this reality. Griff's father was a laborer at the local steel mill, and his mother was a janitor in the elementary school. Although he was known to be an alcoholic, Griff's father was also known to be a caring and giving man who made sure that his wife and six children had the necessities. He especially loved his baby boy, Griff, and often talked about how he knew that Griff would one day grow up and do great things.

Somehow, in spite of the encouragement from his father, mother, and older siblings, Griff got off on the wrong track and began hanging around the gang-bangers, dope addicts, and stick-up artists in the neighborhood. His grades began to suffer. Cutting class led frequently to cutting school altogether. As Griff moved beyond his senior year of high school, he was horrified to find he had lost control of his young life. Griff woke up one morning and realized he had become everything he thought he never would be—a drug addict and an alcoholic. After his mother and father died, Griff went into a free fall, and he ended up among the community's homeless.

"Yo, man, I heard you were going to be buying this liquor store," Griff slurred as he clumsily attempted to open the door of Robert's car. "Boy, I sure hope you do. Then I know I'd have somebody on the inside that could sho'nuff hook me up with a little taste now and then."

Robert jumped out the car and smiled. "Man, can I get a hug first before you start asking me about business?"

As the two old friends embraced, Robert thought about all the blessings that God had showered him with over the past five years. Unlike Griff, Robert, though always a part of the neighborhood gang, avoided the wrongdoings that feed juvenile delinquency. He possessed a different dream. Robert wanted a nice home in the suburbs, a wife, and children. He also wanted to own his own business and control his own destiny. He didn't like the way others treated him when he worked in "their" businesses.

An entrepreneur had given Robert his first big break in business. Tom Hoffman, a successful real estate developer, taught Robert about being successful in real estate. Tom, a white man raised in the deep south, took a liking to Robert and treated him like a son. Robert, eager to be successful, paid close attention to what Tom taught him and learned quickly. Before long Robert was ready to launch his own real estate development business, with the financial backing of Tom. Robert had learned well, and his business grew quickly and became well-known within the region.

"Man, I heard you got big money, Robbo, and that you're looking to invest some of it in the neighborhood." Griff put his arm around Robert and walked him up to the front of the liquor store that was for sale.

"Griff, I don't know who you heard that from. I'm just a poor little colored boy trying to make it in the world. Remember what we used to say as teenagers, 'It's yo' world. I'm just a squirrel, tryin' to get a nut!'" The two men laughed until their eyes watered.

Robert broke off the laughter and quickly interjected, "But you know, Griff, I am interested in buying the liquor store. I've seen the past financials of the business, and it's a profitable operation." Robert's lecture on finance was clearly lost on the intoxicated Griff. And seeing his old buddy in this lost state made Robert have a change of heart.

"You know, Griff, I've already put a deposit down on the business and have first rights of refusal," Robert whispered as he observed the multitude of people entering and exiting the crowded liquor store. As Robert stood on the sidewalk outside the store in the chill autumn air, perplexed about what direction he should take, the answer to his dilemma was being paraded right in front of his eyes. Coming in and out of the liquor store, looking like death, were Johnny, Fat Rat, Black Moses, Bojack, Bootsy, and Jerome. These were all childhood buddies who had become trapped in the world of alcoholism and whose lives were headed nowhere.

Robert turned to Griff. "Man, I've seen enough. I can't do this deal. I'm going to get back my downpayment on Monday."

Griff, who was obviously disappointed, leaned forward, gave Robert a tight hug, and whispered in his ear, "You always were a good homeboy. I think the good Lord has his eye on you. I'll catch you when you come back through the 'hood."

Wisdom to Take Away

- The almighty dollar isn't. Many entrepreneurs spend too much faith, time, and energy trying to appease the money god. Wealth can be either a blessing or a curse depending upon whether or not you must compromise your values to earn it.
- Entrepreneurs must factor their value system into business decisions. For example, don't open a video store that rents adult videos if that conflicts with your moral values.
- Although the object of being a marketer in the marketplace is to gain, remember what can be lost in the process and protect that which is important to you. Each individual is only an event or two away from disaster.

30

The Principle of Bidirectional Intelligence Flow

The Bottom Man at the Top

Mayo Blount had been impressed with the glitzy brochures that the recruiter gave him when KEMET, the large chemical company, came to North Carolina to recruit engineers. Mayo was a country boy, raised on a farm, and had no experience in how to function in a large corporation. Yet he was happy to be considered for the position. After many rounds of interviews, Mayo was offered an engineering assignment at the company's headquarters in Wilmington, Delaware.

The first thing that struck Mayo was that he was the only African American engineer on the staff. Although his teammates were respectful and cordial in front of him, his instincts told him that things were not all that they seemed. He also noticed that most of the black employees were either janitors or mailroom clerks. There were very few black professionals and even fewer black engineers.

The blacks in menial jobs were also treated with disrespect and in some cases contempt. The janitors were especially looked down upon by the few black professionals. And most of the young engineers and white professionals didn't even recognize the janitors or acknowledge their presence when they entered the room to empty the trashcans and vacuum the floors.

Mayo was appalled at this treatment. He had been taught since his youth to honor elderly black men and women but, more important, to respect all people because they were God's creation. His daddy taught him never to judge or value a man by his job title or position but instead by his character and the fruits of his labor. Therefore, Mayo often went out of his way to speak to and show respect for the elderly black janitors in his office building. He not only spoke to them but also took the time to get to know them. He learned about their spouses, their children, their hobbies and interests, their finances, and their hopes and fears.

He looked forward to these conversations because after spending the day dealing with his white coworkers, he found it relaxing and comforting to talk with a black person. Little did Mayo realize that his relationship with the janitors would pay dividends for his career.

Around the time he began these interactions, he noticed that his white coworkers were socializing more after work but usually not inviting him. He also discovered that career-enhancing and confidential company information was being passed around among his white peers but rarely was shared with him.

In time, Mayo became fearful of the consequences of not being in the mainstream of the office's informal network and information channels. One evening while he was working late in the office on the design of a new chemical processing plant, one of the janitors knocked on Mayo's office door. "Mayo, excuse me for bothering you, but I'd like to discuss something with you. Do you have a minute?"

"By all means, Ron, come on in," Mayo responded.

"Mayo, I was cleaning the main conference room on the third floor, and your boss as well as Meredith, Charles, John, and Baxter were in the middle of an intense meeting. I told them that I would come back later, but they insisted that I come in to finish my work. They continued with their meeting, and to my surprise they're talking about upcoming promotions when your name comes up."

Mayo brightened. He had thought he might be in line for a promotion.

"You should know that of all the people in the room, only your boss, Baxter, and Meredith supported your promotion. The other two—Charles and John—were against it and felt you had not shown enough leadership yet. Both said that if you began taking more responsibility, they would then support your promotion."

Mayo was shocked because he had felt that both Charles and John were two of his major supporters. Whenever he had one-on-one meetings with either of these senior managers, both men encouraged him and told him what an outstanding job he was doing. Not once did they indicate that they thought he had not exhibited strong leadership skills. Although disappointed at the new information, Mayo was grateful to Ron because he now had the intelligence he needed to formulate his strategy for getting promoted. He knew exactly what he had to do.

During Mayo's tenure at the company, Ron and others on the janitorial staff occasionally shared with Mayo new information about matters they had observed and heard during evening cleaning. He learned about new projects being considered, which engineers were or weren't favored, and even about who was or wasn't happy at the company. Through this informal network, Mayo received information from the top down and from the bottom up, which in his mind put him in an enviable position.

Mayo became one of the most successful minority executives at the firm before leaving to launch his own business. Since that time he has always recognized those who help him achieve. Mayo understands their value, and now they add to his.

Wisdom to Take Away

- Most companies, governments, and organizations in general have a hierarchical structure that is used to manage the entity. Each position in the company, though varied in size and function, plays a critical role in allowing the organization to meet its stated mission and objectives. Every person in every position in the organization has value. The organization or company is as strong as the weakest of its links.

- Successful entrepreneurs know that because everyone in an organization is valuable and contributes in a unique way, they must seek out and make allies of as many of these people as possible. These people could be as low as janitors or as high as CEOs, but whatever their position, they can either help or hinder your progress. Typically these people will have access to or be privy to important facts that could determine one's level of success or failure. Likewise, entrepreneurs should work to provide information to other members of the organization that may need help. This bidirectional intelligence flow serves to benefit everyone involved.

The Principle of Playing Dumb

The Blackberry Preserves

Vonda Little had been in the events-planning industry since high school. Vonda, always the social butterfly, felt certain about her career plan. First, she would get a degree in hospitality management. Then she would take a job with a hotel to practice handling large budgets and guest lists. Finally, she would open a small business providing the service to local clubs or organizations.

In less than six years, she had accomplished many of her goals. She resigned her hotel job and began devoting the bulk of her time to servicing her local area. Her company, Events by Vonda, had taken off in its first four months, and Vonda hired additional staff to handle smaller projects. The marketplace seemed to have endless opportunities.

Vonda could see only open road before her. But many open roads narrow as they near their destinations, and Vonda wanted to make sure she stayed on the path.

She could see that her blossoming business might take the wrong turn if she focused too heavily on the smaller gatherings. The large parties usually came with contracts that validated her capability. Vonda loved to exceed the client's expectations. She enjoyed adding extra touches. Sometimes she would throw in amenities for a party such as small gift bags that, of course, contained her business card and video. She was a stern dealmaker and was able to secure low prices from her suppliers.

Vonda was fast becoming a force in the industry. Soon she began petitioning for larger projects with larger companies.

Peterson & Beckman, the most prestigious law firm in her native Philadelphia, was planning a large venture. She'd heard through the industry grapevine that none of her competitors would even try for it because the contact for the event, Gary Foster, was notoriously difficult. His reputation preceded him. Gary openly resented anyone who contravened his express wishes, even to make an event more notable. He looked upon such acts as underhanded and treasonous. He was impossible to please.

Vonda was not about to let his reputation for tyranny stop her. If she could accommodate Gary, the news would surely reach other businesses in the area. The only dilemma was how to please a man who did not want to be pleased. Vonda also knew that Gary preferred working with men— white men like himself.

Vonda sent Gary a gift basket left over from a party to begin the appeal. She scouted his interests through a good friend at his agency as well as Gary's assistant. She filled the basket with his favorites, plus her business card and a video package (which contained snippets from successful parties). Then she waited.

Two days later, Gary called. He seemed suspicious—and perhaps rightly so, since she was the only local event planner trying for the job.

"I guess this basket is supposed to persuade me to go with your company," he sniped.

"No, I just want you to know I'm available, Gary. No ulterior motives here," she defended. Vonda could tell that his suspicion was a way to keep her at bay in case she was over-confident about his call.

"Well, just in case you do have ulterior motives, I want you to know that our company is very particular about our business associations." Vonda could hear him tearing open the plastic on the basket. She decided to be honest.

"You know, Gary, I would love to do business with you. I think I could help you out. Why not do things cooperative-ly? Instead of coming up with party schematics, I would prefer to work with your ideas."

He fell silent. Vonda figured one of two things had occurred: He had either discovered the jar of blackberry preserves from Paula's Preserves (his favorite), or he was thinking about what she had said.

"Work with my ideas?" he asked, still slightly suspicious.

"Yes, of course. I believe you know what your company requires. There's no reason for me to design a party that either underserves or overserves your needs. As an event planner, I feel my job isn't to throw a gathering but to tailor one to your specifications." Vonda knew she was striking a chord with Gary. She wanted to convince him that she would not overstep his boundaries.

"You make sense, Vonda, but how can I be sure you'll go with my ideas about the party? How do I know you'll give me what I want?" Just then, he discovered the blackberry preserves. "Are these Paula's Preserves?" he marveled.

Vonda knew he had the answer to his question about business in the small dark purple jar. She landed the job.

Wisdom to Take Away

- The principle of playing dumb is all about balance and instinct. The balancing happens when you want your customer to acknowledge and appreciate your high level of accomplishment and competence in your area of expertise without appearing threatening, condescending, or arrogant. The sad fact is that a few white males are still threatened by an articulate, highly educated, and ambitious woman or minority professional. Some feel so threatened that they may not even engage a minority-owned business in contract opportunities.

- Playing dumb does not mean belittling yourself or not using all your skills. Instead, it means putting the needs of your customer first. For example, when helping your customer to solve a problem, put your best resources on the problem to solve it quickly, understand the politics of your customer's environment and his predicament, present the solution to your customer (make sure the solution is thorough), then step back and let the customer lead.
- The wisdom in these situations is that you must learn when to let people know how smart you are and when to "play dumb," not "be dumb."

32

The
Boomerang Principle

A Kindness Repaid

Trevor James had overcome the stereotype of the "angry black man." After college, he had decided to give back to his community. Socializing had been easy for him in high school, since he ran with the in crowd. In college, he garnered the Big Man on Campus award two years in a row. Even his early career in public relations supported his natural ability to put people at ease. When he opened TJ & Associates as a side business, he never dreamed how his communicative gift would benefit him.

The small things mattered to him. At business lunches, he impressed clients with his courtesy toward the servers. He was on a first-name basis with many people. He once won an account, in the words of his client, "by just being you." That was easy enough; Trevor was an incredible person in all ways. For conferences, he tailored the snacks to match everyone's favorite treat, another small gesture that seemed to help his business.

Eventually, Trevor's side business became his primary business. He increased the size of his staff almost immediately. In three weeks, TJ & Associates included seven PR professionals and three office staff. Unlike many businesses that had started up in the same market, Trevor's company saw a profit befitting a business near its prime. His secret joy was in knowing that a positive outlook and gift for communicating were cornerstones of his success.

Still, TJ & Associates was not invulnerable. One meeting with a potential client was nearly the undoing of Trevor's confidence.

Harrison Leather Goods had acquired several small manufacturers and wanted to improve its image. With more resources and capital available, it was fast becoming the leader in the local marketplace. Trevor and Jeff Maxwell, his long-term employee, wanted to land the account.

Since Harrison Leather was so large, Trevor decided to withhold no expense: the finest restaurant, the best wine, even an after-lunch massage (in which those in the PR business like to indulge). Trevor tended to his guests' every need and wish. Still, he was distracted, thinking about other affairs. Harrison Leather apparently was unimpressed. After two days, there was no response.

When Trevor reviewed events, he knew he had given the lunch too much weight. He spent too much. He fawned too much. He wasn't his natural self.

He called his contact at Harrison Leather, Jennifer Winston. Jennifer owed him a favor and they had a long relationship of helping each other.

"Hey, Trevor, what's up?" Her casualness eased him, but not enough.

"I was hoping to hear from you. Is everything okay or maybe I can do something . . ." he began nervously.

"Relax, Trevor, things went fine the other day. Well, except for one thing. One of the partners didn't believe you were sincere enough. He took the whole expensive lunch thing as an attempt to buy the account. I know you, but . . . "

"I understand." He had lost the account.

"But I was going to say we can still use your group. I convinced him you're the best for the job. Besides, I owe you one." She never missed a beat. Jennifer must have been waiting to tell him this.

"Great! So, we'll talk soon?" He was exhilarated. Still, the good news did not shake his realizations. He ended the conversation politely, as usual.

Trevor was thankful that he had the ability to see his mistakes and that the kindness he'd shown to Jennifer boomeranged into kindness shown him.

Wisdom to Take Away

- The boomerang principle is synonymous with the biblical principle of "as a man sows, so shall he reap." As an entrepreneur, you will find that everything you do comes back at you in similar fashion. For example, if you give to customers, they will give back to you. If you pay people compliments, they will ultimately repay you with a compliment.

- A corollary to this principle is that when you "throw the boomerang"—when you initiate an action (either positive or negative) that may impact one or many people—when it comes back at you, the return impact will be manyfold that of the initial action. For example, if you help someone in business (for example, extend a business loan to someone everyone else has turned down), and then years later you find yourself in a similar predicament, your help will come, but it will far exceed the help you initially provided. Conversely, if you are dishonest and unscrupulous in your business dealings, at some point you will become the victim of numerous business attacks of increased severity and intensity.

33

The Principle of Decision-Node Intelligence

The English Teacher

Tyler Scott, head of Scottsgod.com, trusted in his spiritual faith to carry him through difficult situations. Whether it was the decision to marry his girlfriend Marla or the decision to change his college major from philosophy to Internet commerce, Tyler placed all his faith in his Lord. It was not always an easy remedy, since faith required patience, which he referred to as "walking on air." His Web site was the result of the weekends he spent as a Big Brother to Kenny, who spent countless hours on the Internet. Kenny's fascination fueled Tyler's idea to create a Web site based on his Christian beliefs for teens and youngsters.

After three months of planning and testing possible site designs, Tyler found himself in a quandary. He could not decide whether to use cartoons or actors for his site. He could fill the site with animated cartoons that told the story of Jesus, or he could take a more modern approach to the Passion Story via computer generations of actors performing various texts. The computer generations were more realistic, but they added an ominous quality that made

Tyler hesitant. His site designer, Sean, supported the more modern approach and argued for it at length, but his reasoning only left Tyler more confused. Tyler wanted a realistic site, but not one that would alienate potential users.

Tyler turned to his faith. It had never failed him before.

The start-up of Scottsgod.com had already been announced on three sites with which he had formed links. He could not simply halt its debut, yet he felt no closer to a decision. Tyler felt as if a great machine was at work. He was overwhelmed. In his nightly prayer, he gave thanks for the daily prayer, which was a petition for clear sight and sure ground.

After a month of prayer, Tyler became weary. He could tell when spiritual fatigue set in. He felt hopeful but removed. It was like being a stranded motorist on the side of a highway at rush hour, with plenty of people around but few making any attempt to help.

One day while shopping, Tyler encountered Mr. Richards, his woodshop teacher in middle school.

"I don't believe my eyes. Is that little Tyler Scott?" Mr. Richards guffawed and yanked Tyler into his arms.

"Mr. Richards, how're things? Still teaching woodshop?"

"You mean you don't remember? I retired the same year you and your friends went off to high school."

Events came back to Tyler in a flash. Mr. Richards had created a student project that became a major business for him within a year. Cabbage Patch Kids cradles littered the woodshop, but sold out in two hours at the school fundraiser. Richards patented the idea and immediately opened a shop selling furniture for dolls.

"Of course. How's the business, Mr. Richards?"

Mr. Richards related the great success he had with doll furniture. "And I owe it all to you kids. You came up with the idea, essentially. You know how it goes—I plant the seed, you water, and God gives the increase. I learned what that really means, too."

Tyler wanted to ask him for advice, but he was afraid to seem needy. He tried a different approach. "Mr. Richards, how did you get into doll furniture, anyway? I mean, we kids just made cradles."

Richards drew back as if he knew he was giving business advice to a young hopeful. "I didn't bother with the cradles for long. I let the business find its feet. I knew the sensation created by the cradles wouldn't make for a business venture, and I was looking for a way out of teaching full-time. I started with the cradles, then I let my customers decide which direction I should take."

Tyler had never heard truer words spoken. Only a nine-foot angel swathed in white would have been closer to a divine revelation. Tyler had his answer.

Wisdom to Take Away

- The principle of decision-node intelligence is related to a science called decision analysis. Decision analysis teaches how to analyze business options logically and then to assess which option to choose. Every decision we make provides a single entry into the next decision node, in that one idea relates to another until we reach a point of understanding. Typically, the output side of a decision node contains multiple choices from which to choose. Although entrepreneurs are free to pick any option as the next branch in the decision tree, they must exercise great diligence and caution in choosing. Failure to make a good choice or the "right" choice could result in a significant setback or even failure.

- The key to enhancing your decision-node intelligence and thus increasing your probability of consistently making good decisions is to learn from those who have already gone through those same decision nodes. A good mentor can provide anecdotal data and experiences to assist you in choosing the right branch and helping you to avoid the pitfalls and the painful waste of precious resources. The principle of decision-node intelligence can be related to the principle of mentoring.

The Brain
Borrowing Principle

The Christmas Window

"Christmas in New York is as multicolored and as whimsi-cal as a July fiesta in Mexico," Lita Jasper told herself every year. She marveled at the lights, displays, and the joyful faces of shoppers passing by her Fifth Avenue boutique window. Her shop, Jasper Custom Leather, specialized in custom-designed high-end leather goods: coats, jackets, even shoes and boots. Her creations were the initial draw, but her customers' word-of-mouth boosted her client base. In less than three years, she had been written up in *W, Women's Wear Daily,* and *Elle.*

But this Christmas season she was having trouble coming up with a creative holiday display for the front window. Usually her pride and joy, the front window lacked inspira-tion. No one was stopping on the street to see it. Her regu-lar customers weren't even mentioning it.

Lita wondered why the design was being ignored. The idea was simple but very festive. She had arranged five mannequins in a party scene, with a small Christmas tree in the background and red walls. Two of the party-goers

were seated holding on their laps fully opened boxes reveal-
ing two of her most attractive pieces. Perhaps the display
wasn't as inspired as she had first thought, Lita concluded.

She had spent seven years as a window dresser for Henri
Bendel and had earned a reputation for cutting-edge work.
Was she being shortsighted now?

Her assistant manager, Darvell Freeman, interrupted
Lita's trance to ask a question for a customer. Lita half
answered, still pulled into her reverie. Darvell laughed to
himself, since he'd seen Lita mentally absent before.

Minutes later, Lita found her voice again. "Darv, what
were you asking me when I was . . . you know."

"Right," he said. "I understand. I was asking you for the
price on the now-sold thigh-high boots—you know, the
ones you were saving for yourself."

"Darvell Lamont Freeman! You sold my boots." Lita was
only half angry. She knew that for the right price she'd sell
them too.

"No need to use my middle name, Hippolyta Lolita
Jasper." He was kidding, but he also knew he got her where
it hurts. She could only laugh. Then he laughed. This was a
usual day in the shop.

"So, what are you going to do about that thing?" Darvell
asked, pointing at the window with disdain.

Lita thought. She could redesign it herself, but she was
busy choosing next season's line, negotiating the deal with
the manufacturer, and working on the Christmas party,
bonuses, and Christmas itself. Lita knew Darv wanted to
redesign the window. He was very creative and eager to take
on additional responsibilities. But Lita was having a tough
time letting go.

"Is this another opportunistic attempt to take over
designing my window, Darv?"

"Red-handed." He was still playful but serious.

He gave a quick over-the-shoulder check of the display
floor as he dug in his heels. Lita admired him, but the win-

dow was such an important part of attracting business. "Darv, you know I adore the quicksand you walk on, but I was a window designer . . . "

"Was." He never needed to say much in arguments, and this was becoming an argument. "You had your day because someone gave you a chance. I want the same thing. You already let me design the floor and wall displays. Now is the time, boss. You know I can do it. If you don't like it, you know I'll stay and make right. Why don't you give me a shot?"

Lita hated impassioned pleas. They were structured to tear at the heartstrings. She sighed. Giving him a shot at perhaps a better design would be saying goodbye to . . . what? she pondered. She didn't need the acknowledgment or to earn merit as a window dresser. She didn't have the time to do another display herself. "Wouldn't it be great if I didn't do it? I could leave early every Sunday, like normal people. I could even have a life or at least a few hours more." Lita had made the decision.

"You've got it," she said to Darvell. "But I need something on the edge, not over the edge. No whips, no ropes, no spikes. Keep it classy."

Lita exhaled. She had not given up her power; she used it to gain more.

Wisdom to Take Away

- There have been many intelligent minority and female entrepreneurs throughout the history of America who have helped make our country the beacon of light to the world that it is. Certainly the names of Madame C. J. Walker, James Forten, William Whipper, Stephen Smith, Reginald Lewis, C. Michael Gooden, Nathan Chapman, and Christopher Williams, to name a few, will go down in history as outstanding entrepreneurs. But alongside the many accolades they will receive will be the fact that their business accomplishments were not realized merely from their raw intelligence. Like every successful entrepreneur, they were forced to rely upon their own brainpower plus that of many other people.

- Individuals do good things. Groups of individuals do great things.
- Entrepreneurs must perfect the skill of allowing smart people to grow and prosper within their organization, and they must understand what it will take to retain these individuals.

The Principle of Managing the Ride

Hold on to Your Hat

John Sheppard's anger was visible. His firm had done an outstanding job on the first architectural contract he won from this client, and John thought the client would be more understanding about the mistake his team had made on the latest job. To John's chagrin, his client was in no mood for mercy.

John blamed himself for the situation. When his company had won the first contract, he concentrated on doing an outstanding job. Everyone knew this was important because the firm had received a long-term deal with options to renew for up to three years. John was proud of how his team of architects and engineers rose to the occasion.

Unfortunately, they began to make mistakes as soon as they became successful. Not only were their egos inflated, but their outflow of cash became inflated as well. To match their perception of how good they were, the team felt compelled to move to larger, more expensive office space. The company leased new cars for the executives and ordered new office equipment. Surveying the impressive skyline of downtown Chicago through the stained-glass windows of his penthouse office suite, John ruefully recalled, "I really felt I had to upgrade our image in order to compete with the big boys."

Two years later John's company bid on another contract with the same client and won it easily because of the firm's reputation. John had to ramp up quickly and begin delivering technical services. Unfortunately, unlike on the first contract, his staff made some significant errors on the design and engineering of the new structures. Although the team caught the mistake before anyone was hurt, great damage was done to the firm's reputation. It wasn't long before members of the client's technical staff began making negative comments about John's company. Worse, the client took steps to nullify the contract.

John's firm went into a tailspin. John had difficulty eating, sleeping, and concentrating on his work. Soon, key personnel began jumping ship, and the company moved ever closer to bankruptcy.

Walking through the now mostly empty office space, John reflected on his experiences over the past two years. "We didn't effectively manage the cycles of business. When business was good, I shouldn't have let that success dictate how we viewed ourselves or how we ran the company. We weren't ready to sustain the growth." He sighed. "Now, while business is tough, I can't allow it to shake my confidence. I'll survive this crisis—and from now on I'll hold on to my hat and manage the ride better."

Wisdom to Take Away

- Successful entrepreneurs recognize that business is just like life—it runs through cycles. Businesses grow and they shrink. They are profitable one year and lose money the next. Your staff performs in an exemplary fashion on one contract and bombs on the next. How you manage these swings is directly proportionate to the company's long-term success.

- Average entrepreneurs adjust their emotions to the swings in the cycle, but successful entrepreneurs calibrate their emotions at midpoint between the highs and the lows. They manage to maintain this equilibrium throughout the entire business journey, despite the changes and vicissitudes of the external environment.

- Even though the external environment continues to move through the cycles, successful entrepreneurs maintain a steady and constant reaction to those changing external events. This steadiness minimizes the emotional and psychological effects that changes can cause, and helps entrepreneurs perform consistently and efficiently over the long term. Steady consistency is indeed a great way to manage the ride.

The You Don't Have Because You Don't Ask Principle

Silent Voices

Shirley Franklin once was a singer, but that was long ago. Now she spent her time teaching the art of song to children. Shirley gained a newfound sense of completeness when she taught students how to breathe, how to carry the feeling into the sound, how to be the music. Yet she never made much of a living at it.

Her son, Jeremy, was a teenager now with all the normal needs and wants that tax the purse of a parent. Suddenly she had a growing sense of financial need. Her late husband was the financial whiz. He made money matters seem so easy. When he died, he left a financial web of stability that included stocks, annuities, mutual funds, and multiple accounts overseen by his former business partner and brother, Harlan. She didn't want to worry about money, but life was becoming increasingly expensive as Jeremy prepared for college.

Shirley knew she had the time and talent required to open a vocal repertory school. The cost of space was not a major concern. The main problem was getting started. It was as if she had all the ingredients for a cake but no recipe. She needed help but was uncertain where to turn.

After attending the recital of one of her students, Shirley was surprised to run into her former vocal coach, Betty Ridgeway, in the park. Shirley had gone there to sit and relax. She and Betty had been friends for ten years and had a strong, trusting bond. Betty hugged her as if they hadn't seen each other in years, although they lunched at least once a month.

Shirley opened up about her situation for the first time. "Betty, I really want to open a rep class. I have all I need—money, location, potential staff . . . "

Betty interrupted, "So, why haven't you gotten started?" Betty disliked excuses.

"I need some business advice—help with the details. But I don't want someone who will come in and try to take over. I'm not sure who to trust."

"How much do you think you're going to have to trust?"

The question rang in Shirley's mind over and over.

"The fact is that no one completely trusts anyone. What you need to trust is yourself. Then you need to ask for help. You can't expect to get very far if you don't use what's available."

Betty was right. Shirley had been unable to make a move because she simply had not asked. She had so many resources—trusted friends, close relatives with business experience, even Harlan, her finance-savvy brother-in-law.

The two lingered a while in the park discussing the rep class. Shirley left feeling reassured about her venture. She realized that she needed to release her feelings of distrust and to ask for help and counsel. The next month, she opened her school with three classes instead of one.

Wisdom to Take Away

- Many times entrepreneurs will go through the process of researching a customer's needs, developing solutions to those needs, documenting and presenting findings to the customer, and then will walk away from the table without asking for the business. This principle makes it clear that whatever outcome you desire, first be diligent about mastering the technical requirements, then ask for what you want in order to get it.
- This principle applies when an entrepreneur is in need of help. When you find yourself in need of help, you must first admit it and then seek out people who can help. You'll be pleasantly surprised at how many busy people are willing to help others if they are asked.

WEEK

37

The T3 Principle

A Small Sacrifice

It was a rainy Tuesday in San Diego, and Cass Thompson had just finished an emergency meeting with her staff of ten to galvanize them for the coming holiday shopping rush. It was early November, and the store, Playing Games, had just received its huge holiday merchandise shipment—and only four hours before closing. Cass had called in the entire crew because she anticipated the late delivery. The stock had to be inventoried and shelved before the games and gadgets and other holiday merchandise would be available for an important holiday sale scheduled for the next morning.

These were important times for the store. It had just reopened in its new Gas Light District location, and it was vital that sales volume increase significantly in the high-stakes Christmas season. After all, rent in this trendy shopping area was astronomical now that new restaurants had opened. Cass had taken a big risk by signing the lease—not many businesses made it in this posh marketplace.

Today's challenge was to set up the merchandise for the sale, but there was so much to accomplish while helping customers at the same time. "The store could close a little early," she figured, "but that would mean a loss of potential business."

Cass concluded that sacrificing a few dollars would be well worth the business she could generate tomorrow if they put in the hard work to prepare for the sale. Cass understood all too well the importance of sacrifice, and she was acutely aware that doing good business meant constant focus and the absence of free time. These were lessons she had learned in college.

Although she was a good student, her college years did not yield a degree. After making it through nearly four years, she found herself pregnant with twins in her senior year. It was a difficult pregnancy, which made schoolwork virtually impossible. She planned to marry the father, but in the end the relationship failed. Dejected but determined, she moved in with friends and gave up on college to have children and go to work to support them.

Four years had passed since those tough times, and she was enjoying success as a mother and an entrepreneur. She had found the perfect nanny in her retired mother and had built up Playing Games enough to find herself in the Gas Light District. The results of her hard work and sacrifice were becoming apparent.

Cass phoned her mom to warn her about the evening. "Mom, I'm sorry, but I'll be pretty late tonight. We just got the shipment from the manufacturer, and it will be quite a few hours before we'll be free." Cass's mom was supportive and understanding.

After the call, she divided up time and tasks among her workers and closed the shop for the day. Tonight's sacrifice would be well worth it to be ready for tomorrow.

Wisdom to Take Away

- Every business will require a certain degree of sacrifice in order to succeed in the long-term.

- Every one of us has been endowed in varying degrees with three valuable assets: time (24 hours a day, 365 days a year), talent (e.g., math, science, music, marketing, writing, speaking), and treasure (various material assets, money, real estate, or other possessions). The combination of these three assets (T3) allows entrepreneurs to leverage growth and creativity. It's important to note that if you're short on treasure, you'll need to depend more upon time and talent in the beginning of your venture.
- The benefit of making the T3 investment is that you can create a system in which one asset bolsters another. By pursuing a particular venture, you may gain more treasure (e.g., money, profits, enhanced net worth).
- The increased treasure, if invested correctly, could free up time to be with family, while the transaction could mean gaining additional marketable skills, which could then translate into more business.

38

The Principle of Building a Stronger Community

There Goes the Neighborhood

Leah Brown was beside herself. Her Jamaican temper was starting to get the best of her. "Can you believe the audacity of Jacob? How dare he call us names behind our backs while smiling to our faces! Then to add insult to injury, he thinks we'll forgive and forget and come shuffling to his party. I'm sure he only invited us to be politically correct, since we're the only two black families in the neighborhood."

John, Leah's husband, watched his love as she vented her frustration about a situation no one was to win. He could only agree while cautiously avoiding anything to fuel her anger. Racism was a battle he had long since stopped fighting with anger. John was a man of quiet desperation. He stared at his dismayed and angered neighbor, Jerry Price.

Leah turned her attention to Jerry. "I'm so angry, Jerry. What are you going to do? Will you accept his invitation after what he said about us?"

Both families had been invited to Jacob's gathering of friends and neighbors. Jerry and Leah shared a friendship and respect, since they shared in the "us" of being black families in the neighborhood.

Jerry found himself in a quandary. Until two weeks ago, he believed he lived in a nice, upper-middle-class neighborhood where homes fell in the $500,000 range with most having three-car garages and over 5,000 square feet of living space. On average, Jerry's and Leah's neighbors were decent people. Leah and John had two children, a boy 12 years old and a 17-year-old daughter set to attend Duke University in the fall. Jerry and his wife, Barbara, had five daughters ranging in age from 6 to 22. Leah was a successful investment banker for a major firm in Washington, D.C., and Jerry was a founder of a growing and very profitable moving and storage company.

Living in a safe and comfortable neighborhood in the suburbs was the realization of a lifelong dream that Jerry had as a young boy in the tough neighborhood of Harlem. His family too was of West Indian descent. Jerry was well versed in the struggles of the poor. He reveled in his heritage of strong, forthright people. Like so many of his brethren, he understood the importance of providing for his family.

After sacrificing a promising career at Disney, Jerry worked hard to build his business up to a point where he could afford a house in the suburbs. He was attracted to this particular neighborhood because of its reputation for having outstanding schools. Although he was excited about the schools, he lamented that his daughters had to deal with the uncomfortable reality of being the only black children in their class.

The dinner conversations with his children often revealed that the schools, though well-intentioned, lacked understanding and appreciation of African American culture. The schools did not celebrate Black History Month, since there were so few blacks enrolled. Their classmates needed education about black America because most parents avoided the subject. Often the lack of understanding escalated into outright hostility toward his children and other children of color.

Despite these concerns, Jerry enjoyed his neighborhood and had grown to admire most of his neighbors. So he was greatly disappointed when he learned that Jacob Levin had made racially insensitive comments about him and his family. Neither Leah nor Jerry believed that Jacob would harbor such sentiments. They assumed that his minority status as a Jew would serve as a restraint on intolerance. The irony of the sorry episode was that another Jewish neighbor, who lived between Jerry and Jacob, exposed the dark side of Jacob.

Mrs. Anna Shapiro explained to Jerry that she was working in her yard when some African American boys came to visit Jerry's daughters. The young men were polite, educated, and respectful—they were posing no apparent threat to anyone. But like most young people, they liked loud music and were blasting their radios while flirting with the girls. Jacob Levin was also in his yard tending to his tulips and became agitated about the presence of the young visitors and annoyed by the loud rap music.

Speaking in Yiddish, Jacob called to his children, who were playing in the street in front of his home. "Children, come into the house. The niggers are at it again!" Jacob didn't realize that Mrs. Shapiro, who was also of Jewish ancestry and fluent in Yiddish, overheard him and was disturbed and surprised by Jacob's racial slur.

Mrs. Shapiro, a proud ex-hippie from the 1960s and an unabashed liberal, immediately notified Jerry's and Leah's families about Jacob's unfortunate lapse in judgment and morality. Jerry was taken aback because he had come to know and like Jacob. Their daughters played on the same soccer and basketball teams, and Jerry had even hosted Jacob and his lovely wife, Susan, at his home for dinner.

As Leah and John sipped on a cup of tea in the Prices' kitchen, she again asked Jerry what they should do about the invitation from Jacob.

"I don't know about you guys, but there is no way I will ever set foot in that man's house again. As a matter of fact, I might even put sugar in his gas tank and slice his tires! Either way, I'll never forgive him for what he said."

Jerry was more hurt than angry. "Leah, although I'm just as bothered by all of this as you are, my religion tells me that I must forgive Jacob, no matter what. If I don't forgive him, then God will not forgive me of my trespasses. I'm not sure if I'll ever forget, but I must certainly try to forgive. Maybe one way to begin the forgiving process would be for me to attend his party, despite his racially insensitive comments.

Leah looked to John for support but found none. He wasn't interested in fighting this fight. "Well, suit yourself, Jerry," Leah said as she placed her unfinished cup of tea in the kitchen sink and made for the door. "I've never been one to be an Uncle Tom, and I'm not planning to start now. I'll talk to you later."

Leah's words cut Jerry like a knife. He had been accused of many things in his life but never of being an Uncle Tom. Yet he stuck with his decision to attend Jacob's party. Dressed in his standard conservative blue blazer, khaki trousers, golf shirt, and penny loafers, Jerry walked up the street to Jacob's house and reluctantly rang the doorbell. He had given his decision more thought and rationalized that he could attend the party, avoid a face-to-face encounter with Jacob, and then make a hasty getaway. But as the door swung open, there stood Jacob, dressed in his blue blazer and khakis.

"Hi, Jerry. I'm so glad you could come. I've been meaning to stop by to see you and Barbara. Please join me in the library for a moment." As Jerry followed Jacob through the throng of guests, he looked to see if any other African Americans had attended. He saw none.

Jacob closed the library door behind him, asked Jerry to sit on the couch, and began to pour out his heart. "Jerry, this is very tough for me, but I have to get it off of my chest. For many nights I've been unable to sleep because of something I said recently that I'm very ashamed of. Jerry, a few weeks ago, I was in my yard and I observed some boys with your daughters. They seemed like decent kids, but they were especially loud and engaged in horseplay. My children were playing near them, so I instructed my kids to come into the house. However, in my anger and fear, I made a racially insensitive comment. I used the word 'nigger.' I said it in Yiddish so no one would know what I said. But Jerry, the moment I said it I knew it was wrong, and it has bothered me day and night. Jerry, I'm so sorry. I wish I could take back what I said. Although I said something racist, I'm not a racist. Would you please forgive me for my stupidity?"

Jerry was dumbfounded. Jacob obviously had no idea that Jerry already knew about the comment, so Jerry was even more moved by Jacob's honesty and remorse. Jerry cleared his throat. "I appreciate your honesty and sincerity, Jacob. I think all of us say and do things in life that we regret and are truly sorry for. I accept your apology, Jacob, and am willing for us to move on together."

"Thank you, Jerry," Jacob responded. "You don't know what a relief it is for me to lift this burden from my heart. Now that I've ruined your evening, let me make it up to you by introducing you to some friends of mine. One guy in particular I want you to meet is William Green. His company—he's the president—is relocating its corporate headquarters, and he's looking for a reputable moving and storage company. I strongly recommended you. It's a large organization, and this could be a sizable contract for you."

Jerry met Mr. Green at the party and ultimately won the contract, which is now the largest contract that Jerry's company manages.

Leah's anger eventually died down. She heard about Jacob's apology and waited for one herself before she would speak to her neighbor. Jacob soon complied.

Wisdom to Take Away

- The road to business success and financial gain is paved with sharp stones. Having a layer of protection often will keep injury at bay. Entrepreneurs must be prepared for a treacherous path.
- When others say harsh things, forgiveness is the only remedy. Forgive yourself for any negativity you feel, and forgive the comment. Many times it has less to do with a person's view that it does with ignorance, which can be remedied, or anger, which fades away with time.

WEEK
39

The Principle of
Spiritual Fortitude

Making It to the Promised Land

Josh never questioned the wisdom of his parents. Growing up in the gritty neighborhood of South Central Los Angeles, he was somehow sheltered from the cruel realities of being poor in the inner city. Despite their low economic status, their blighted neighborhood, and the pervasive hopelessness of the people in the community, Josh's parents maintained a remarkable sense of hope in the future. They believed in the principles of democracy and the pursuit of happiness that were integral to the American experience. His parents ingrained in Josh and his siblings the idea that the best and brightest always win and ultimately will rise to the top.

Josh excelled in school. He was consistently an A student while lettering in three varsity sports. He never got in trouble with the law, and he avoided the violent gangs that terrorized his neighborhood. He was generally recognized as a promising young African American male who had a very bright future.

When Josh was seventeen, his positive attitude and excellent performance in school attracted serious scrutiny from

MIT's school of engineering. At that time, the school was interested in diversifying its student body and was seeking young, bright students like Josh to join its academic family. Grateful for the opportunity, Josh and his parents agreed that he would attend MIT and major in computer science engineering.

As predicted, Josh excelled in his academic pursuits— even MIT was not difficult for him. After receiving a bachelor's degree in engineering, he earned an MBA from Harvard Business School and began a promising career as an executive-in-training at a large information-technology company.

Josh's parents had taught him to believe in the meritocracy of America, but they also taught him to be self-sufficient and to be captain of his own destiny. Even though he had a great job, Josh longed for a spot where he could call the shots and have greater input. Josh wanted to launch his own business.

Starting a business in the information-technology industry proved to be relatively easy for Josh. Each month, he put aside 20 percent of his earnings as seed capital to invest in his business. Equally important, he built an impeccable reputation as an astute engineer and as a person with high morals and strong character. People believed and liked Josh. Consequently, he was successful at rapidly attracting new customers and building an impressive pipeline of business opportunities. Josh's company became known for top-quality technical work, a well-trained engineering staff, and a high degree of professionalism.

It was against this backdrop that Josh decided to bid on a lucrative federal contract at the Department of Defense (DOD) to provide telecommunications services at various military bases across the country. This multimillion-dollar contract, if won, would span at least five years and provide the financial foundation that would support significant growth at the firm for years to come. Josh's company had

done work for the DOD before and had established an outstanding reputation.

But in preparing to respond to the Request for Proposal
(RFP), Josh began to sense some animosity from the government officials who were responsible for the process. This
was puzzling in light of the mutually beneficial relationship
he had established with the DOD over the years. Still, he
couldn't put his finger on what was wrong. Josh responded
to the RFP.

Josh was confident that his costs, project plan, and proposed management team were highly competitive and provided the client the best deal. But, despite this strong position, his firm was abruptly disqualified in the first round of
competition. This meant he was precluded from participating in the "best and finals" for this particular bid.

Josh was mortified. "How could this happen?" he kept
asking himself. He was the incumbent on the contract. He
had employed the best engineers that money could buy.
Research showed that his cost was consistently competitive
in the telecommunications industry, and besides, he had
been led to believe that he had the inside track. Something
was wrong. When Josh and his team met to discuss what
had happened, he kept repeating, "We deserved to win this
business. This is not right."

After many sleepless nights, he decided to protest the
decision and solicited the support of a powerful business
advocate.

Protesting the contract award was a difficult undertaking.
It was a drain on cash flow due to the high legal costs. It
was also a drain on the firm's time, since the management
team had to spend long hours meeting with the legal team.
There was also the possibility that Josh's firm might be
blackballed from the DOD. Although protesting federal
contract decisions is legal and an accepted practice, some
government representatives resent being challenged by an
outside vendor. These officials have the power to make it

almost impossible for the vendor to do business in that agency again. Last, protesting the contract award was an emotional drain on Josh. The process required so much of his time and energy that other functions of his company began to suffer.

Despite these setbacks, and with the help of the minority-business advocacy group, Josh pushed ahead. They fought the decision for several difficult years. Many times the only thing that kept Josh going was his belief that the universe was on his side and that he deserved to win. Five years later the review board ruled in Josh's favor.

Wisdom to Take Away

- In our universe there are two types of events—events that we control and events that are outside of our control. The principle of spiritual fortitude suggests that entrepreneurs focus on the events within their control and leave the uncontrollable events to the wisdom of the universe. The universe ultimately rewards those who consistently add value.
- Successful minority entrepreneurs acknowledge the power of spiritual fortitude. Not to be confused with any religion, spiritual fortitude reflects the individual's ability to influence the forces of the universe to act on his or her behalf. Recognizing this universal force, allowing it to influence your decisions, and testing its power are the critical steps to wielding the power of spiritual fortitude.

The Ownership Principle

The Pity Party

Whenever Erika Taylor had a problem, she faced it head on without trepidation, without fear. For all her courageous resolve, she could not shake her current dilemma. The temporary agency she owned, AbleBodies, was in the red. There was blight in the business sector of her native Charlotte, North Carolina. Many of the large companies headquartered in the area were adjusting their corporate structure to include working from home or using the Internet to transact business. Temp agencies all over were suffering. Erika locked herself in her office to think.

AbleBodies had a foundation of long-standing clients that kept it operational, but the blight was taking its toll on even that. Erika began her business because as a "career temp" she came to learn the ins and outs of agencies. At her last agency, she learned the most important element to starting her business: need. At the time, the major corporations had just arrived and were understaffed. Erika had worked as a temp for about six years, often as a receptionist. She realized that the paperwork was more task-driven than technically complex. She knew several other temps looking for assignments.

AbleBodies had enjoyed a strong three-year run since its inception. Erika was overbooked more than once. She increased the size of her staff nearly tenfold. She never had a losing year. Her entire staff was working on assignment. It was too good to last.

During the fourth year, the downturn began. IBM pulled out first, then Bell Atlantic. She panicked but never let it show. She was never one to run scared. She began a cold-calling and promotional campaign to appeal to smaller businesses in the area. It produced a few small contracts but nothing compared to the business she had lost. She put a freeze on hiring, deciding to stick with the 81 temps she now supported.

The small contracts and the remaining large accounts kept her afloat until the fifth year. Erika saw Beatrice, Nabisco, and two large advertising firms pull up stakes. Erika faced the future with great uncertainty. She could not guarantee jobs for half her temps. She knew most were employed by more than one agency, but the slump was sure to have a blanket effect. She felt helpless.

Erika called her assistant, Ray, into her office. He always gave straight answers. She wanted a straight talk about the future of the business. Ray had been with her from the start and was like a partner. He would tell her if she was missing some crucial piece of logic. He had more business education than she did, and she had intended to make him a partner in the fifth year had things gone well.

"Wondering what to do, huh?" Ray was intuitive. He knew his boss and friend well.

She enjoyed his attempts at telepathy. "Good guess. Ray, things are not looking great around here, you know that. If another big account goes, we're going to have to cut corners." She still wanted to sound confident, as if she had a plan.

"We've already cut so many corners that we made a circle, Erika." He laughed. "What are we going to do, make double-sided copying mandatory?" He chuckled again, amused at himself.

"I'm serious and you know that. Ray, we were in the red last quarter. We can't keep that up. I just wish those corporations hadn't deserted me. I feel we're out of options." Erika sank in her chair.

"I suppose you want me to invite the others?" Ray seemed unaffected by her tirade.

"For what?"

"The pity party you're throwing for yourself. I know things look bad, but you found your way to success initially. Now you have a setback and you're preparing for Armageddon. It's not that critical. Being in the red doesn't mean staying there. We won't hire for a while, maybe even weed out the undesirables around here in the process."

He was right, as usual. She'd make him a partner now if she could. "I guess you're right. I shouldn't blame myself. It isn't my fault they left."

"Wait a minute, Erika. You of all people know you are just as responsible for your reaction as they are for their action."

"How?" She failed to grasp his point.

"You run the show, so you are responsible not for what you can't change but for what you can. The prayer of serenity, you know." Ray had a way of hitting the nail on the head.

From that moment Erika realized she needed to be proactive. She had taken ownership of the problem. Now she would take ownership of solving it.

Wisdom to Take Away

- Entrepreneurs who blame other people and other things for their failures are in essence passing the power to solve their problems on to someone else. Successful entrepreneurs, when faced with challenges and setbacks, first look inward to assess what they could have done either to avoid or to mitigate the challenges and problems that confront them. For example, imagine an entrepreneur makes a sales call on someone who turns out to be racist. The entrepreneur cannot control the fact that the person is bigoted, but he can certainly take ownership of the situation and figure out ways to use that bigotry against the person or to minimize the impact of it on him and his company.

- Failure to take ownership of a problem eats away at your problem-solving capability. The ownership principle suggests that you take control and ultimate ownership of every aspect of your life. Though you may not have caused the problem, you must take ownership of finding the solution to the problem.
- This principle also suggests that the more ownership you take for solving your problems, the more problems you'll be able to solve. Further, you'll be able to solve them more quickly, and their level of complexity will diminish.

41

The Mental Triad Principle

The Sunday Morning Sermon

Pastor Randolph Stephens was a gifted speaker and spiritual counselor. He spoke from the heart and touched the congregants who listened to him this Sunday morning. His sermonic notes were more of a guide than the "thou shalt and shalt nots." He believed in following the spirit rather than the program. Thus, all Sunday sermons started punctually, but they ended at whatever time he finished speaking. Pastor Stephens had a large and diverse congregation with an unusually high percentage of entrepreneurs. Perhaps it was his own entrepreneurial drive that motivated the parishioners. Stephens maintained two small businesses.

This morning he focused on helping his church to move to a place of peace by understanding the three components of self and how they operate.

"You must understand that the combined self is a being unto itself. The self can be selfish. It disregards God's principles to fulfill the flesh. You must learn to recognize which part of the combined self is in operation at the moment or you will be doomed to follow its every whim, even its whim not to come to church. "

Parishioner Talma Regent squirmed in her chair. She was a respected seamstress who occasionally charged astronomical prices when she was financially strapped.

"First, there is the self of the world—that physical being that feels and perceives. It is the seat of your emotions. That's why you've got to have that cigarette when you're depressed, or that drink. This emotional component needs to be controlled more than any other."

Quinton Starks, the organist, shifted uneasily. He canceled lessons with his students when his fiancée and he fought. He was driven by his emotions.

"Then you have to learn to recognize the self of the mind. Your knowledge that puffs you up. Your wisdom that overshadows those around you. Some of us are guilty of the sin of following the self of the mind, following our intellect into what is logically sound, what fits the equation when God's love cannot be measured by any equation."

Reggie Mack, his assistant pastor, winced with recognition. He, too, was an entrepreneur owning a company that built customized PCs. He was also a know-it-all who used his knowledge of computers to coerce customers to buy certain packages that were more expensive than necessary.

"Finally, church, I want to encourage you by talking about the most hopeful and promising part of the self. It is the part that loves without question or fear. It is the part that knows where to find peace in time of trouble: the spiritual self. The spirit can abide no matter the evil you face. But it must be cultivated, nurtured with truth, fed the Word. You cannot hope to make it in this dark world if you do not know your spirit."

There was a collective sigh from the crowd. Pastor Stephens reached them where they were in their current spiritual journeys. His words especially blessed the many businessmakers in the congregation. Their struggle touched his own. He knew this and its potential impact, but Pastor Stephens had to speak from the heart.

Wisdom to Take Away

- Entrepreneurs are most effective when they have per-
  fected the three selves of the human condition. These
  three selves are the emotional self, the intellectual
  self, and the spiritual self.
- Emotional stability sounds like a mantra from a New
  Age tome, but successful people must develop a sense
  of having solid ground under their feet even when
  they are free-floating. The emotional self requires this
  grounding to be of use.
- Intellect is certainly a part of the mental triad, but it is
  by no means the only component. The intellectual
  self is maximized only when the entrepreneur successfully combines the modules of intellect, knowledge,
  and wisdom. A strong intellect and the lifelong accumulation of knowledge require wisdom, which is the
  ability to discern inner qualities and relationships
  resulting in a wise attitude or course of action. All
  parts should be used concurrently.
- The spiritual self is our guide—our "small voice"—
  that advises us on paths of truth.

WEEK
42

The Principle of Internalized Oppression

The Trip to Ghana

The thirteen-hour flight from New York to West Africa was draining. The four-hour drive from the airport in Accra, Ghana, to the remote village of Bekwai was torturous. Joyce had been tossed and rattled so much that every muscle in her body ached. She was grateful when she and the 32 other missionaries finally reached their destination shortly before sunset.

The houseboy, Kwami, greeted them. "You're lucky," he said. "Tonight we have electricity. You will not have to unpack in the dark."

Kwami closed and locked the gate behind the bus. The steel barrier shut out the dank houses and poverty that existed just beyond the brick walls of the compound. As the men started unloading the luggage, Joyce could feel her legs and arms tingle. She was unsure if the sensation was due to renewed circulation or to anxiety tinged with the excitement she felt about the upcoming experience.

Unlike the other members of her group, Joyce would have preferred to stay at the compound to rest. Unfortunately, the

Ashanti village chief had insisted that all of the Americans meet at the church for a welcoming celebration with the villagers. "I can't be rude and refuse such an invitation on our first night here," she thought. Weary, reluctant, but sensitive to the ancient customs of her Ghanaian hosts, Joyce boarded the church bus and made her way to the ceremony.

The Americans entered the church, and the pastor ushered them past rows and rows of backless wooden benches crowded with the villagers. The custom of the Ashanti was to have guests sit in the front of the church facing the congregation. Joyce took a seat and found herself looking at a group of more than 800 curious Ghanaians. As she studied the warm, friendly, intelligent faces, her anxiety melted and she began to relax.

The village chief stood, gestured for silence, and began. "We want to welcome these Americans to our village. They have come to help build our church. Although they are very tired from their travels, they have agreed to meet with you and to answer any questions you have. Before we begin, we will ask them to introduce themselves."

One by one, the missionaries went to the microphone; their comments were translated for the congregation. Among the group were entrepreneurs, teachers at a Seventh Day Adventist church school, computer science engineers, doctors, and nurses. With each introduction the audience's interest and enthusiasm increased. When it was her turn, Joyce explained that she was a communications specialist and owned her own marketing communications firm in downtown Atlanta.

After the introductions, the congregation began to ask questions: "What do you Americans think of Ghana so far?" asked one. "How do you share your money in America when the husband and wife both work?" asked another. "Why is the divorce rate so high in America?" "Your children are so big. What do they eat?" they wanted to know.

The warm, God-loving nature of the Ashanti people poured forth as they asked whatever questions came to mind.

It was close to midnight when the questions started to die down. "We know our guests are tired," the chief said. "We can have only one more question."

From the rear of the church an elderly man motioned that he owned the final question. He appeared to be well into his eighties, with a face the color of sweet dark chocolate, and he wore traditional garb—a colorful Kente wrap. The man was obviously highly respected in the village, because when he stood to speak the entire church paused. Mothers quieted the restless children seated on their laps. Others hissed to direct all attention to the speaker.

"I think that I speak for all the members of our village when I say that we're glad you're here and appreciate that you've come 8,000 miles to build a church for our village. All of your backgrounds are very impressive. As I listened to you introduce yourselves, I was impressed. I heard that among you there are doctors, nurses, businessmen, teachers, and engineers. How will you build a church when none of you are a carpenter or a brickmason."

The church was still, waiting for someone to respond to the old man. Joyce questioned herself. "You know, he makes a good point. I have no experience in construction. The most I have done is to install wallpaper in my bathroom. What am I doing here, anyway? We have no credentials to do what we say we're here to do."

The chief, fearing that one of their own may have insulted the guests, asserted that he knew God would bless everyone's efforts. Work would begin at 6:00 the next morning.

On the short ride back to the compound, the leader of Joyce's group sensed the lingering doubt in the missionaries' minds and gave a pep talk. He encouraged them to challenge all of their paradigms about what they were or were not capable of doing. He reminded them that the collective skills of the missionaries and the Ghanaians were sufficient to do God's work.

Weeks later, Joyce was back in the states having lunch with a business associate and enthusiastically describing her African experience. "I wouldn't have believed it myself if I hadn't been there. Our first day on the construction site, over one hundred Ghanaian people came to help us build the church. Although most couldn't speak English and we couldn't speak their language, we cut and sawed and hammered and nailed together. I learned to make mortar by mixing sand, concrete, and water—and by the third day I was laying bricks! Smoothing that mortar over a layer of bricks was like spreading icing on a giant sheet cake. Everyone chipped in and we built that church in six days! On the seventh day, the Sabbath Day, we worshiped.

"There were so many people who thought we couldn't do it. I'll never forget how the old man questioned our ability to construct the building. You know what else? Helping to build that church taught me a lesson about myself, my own capabilities, and how I run my business, how I choose new employees. I've rejected applicants just because they didn't have exactly the credentials I thought they needed, even though they had years of related experience. From now on, whenever I interview people, I'll look past credentials to see what skills and experience they can bring."

Wisdom to Take Away

- Too often people miss out on a major opportunity because they think they lack the credentials. As a result, they become victims of their own internalized oppression: They operate under a belief system that disregards the value they can add, the accomplishments they have achieved.
- Successful entrepreneurs look past the papers and degrees, understanding that credentials are not the

only indicators of a person's talents and skills. Successful entrepreneurs create environments that stress the importance of continuous learning. When people are free to demonstrate what they know and are encouraged to learn what they don't know, their value to the team increases dramatically.

43

The Principle of Forgiveness

The True Believer

Carmen Esposito sat at the conference table in awe. She had never expected to be insulted. That assumption seemed only natural, since she had maintained a long and positive relationship with Colco, Inc., one of her best accounts. Yet here she was being berated for her personal views on religion. Her spirituality rested on traditional beliefs she learned as a child. She practiced the African religion of Ifa, called Santeria in the Americas. Carmen had refrained from such discussions in the past, but the meeting took a turn she was unable to avoid.

Michael Nelson, her Colco contact, was a staunch Christian. He truly liked her and mentioned more than once that his personal feelings about her kept her in good stead with his company. When he suggested that her company join his in backing a church's fundraiser, she recoiled. It ran counter to so many of her beliefs. She didn't disdain Christianity. In fact, she thought of herself as a liberal who did not discount the beliefs of others. Most of her accounts were with companies whose employees were predominately Christian. There had never been a problem before, but she had never been in this position before either.

Michael had detected her reluctance to participate and went on the attack. "How could anyone not want to back a fundraiser for a church?" he exclaimed.

Carmen was afraid to answer. She didn't want to offend him, so at first she skirted the issue. "I'm sure your company can handle the fundraiser," she said.

Michael was eyeing her warily. She struggled to form a better answer. "Listen, Michael, I want to be honest with you. It's not that I don't believe in God or anything like that. It's just that I never envisioned my company involved in religious activities. Besides, I wouldn't want to upset any of my clients who may not be Christian."

She believed she was safe. Michael seemed momentarily satisfied with her answer. She tried to change the subject. "Why don't we move on to other matters?"

Jay Huff, Michael's partner, chimed in. "I don't want to offend you, Carmen, but why would you think your other clients would be upset that you backed a Christian fundraiser? Surely, even your Muslim clients wouldn't object to such an idea. It benefits people."

Carmen was not off the hook. She tried again. "Please, fellas, let's move on. I don't want to argue religion today." She was practically pleading.

Michael was still bothered. "You know, Carmen, I'd swear it was you with the problem, not your clients." He was on to her.

"Fine, then. I'm not a Christian, all right?"

"No, not all right. Our company was founded on Christian morals and tenets." His words cut.

"I am a believer, okay? I'm just not a Christian. My family is from Cuba. I was brought up on Santerian beliefs. Many coincide with Christianity, I hear."

"But they aren't Christian." Jay Huff was no longer on her side. The factions were building around her. Michael maintained his look of disapproval. He was upset with her, as if she had disappointed him somehow—this after liking her for so long.

"I'm sorry, Carmen, but your revelation concerns me. I can't believe you're some kind of pagan or heathen. It's like playing for the losing team at final judgment."

That was the insult she could not get past. Michael and Jay had lost respect for her. She knew this moment could end their business relationship. And it did. Only hours after the meeting, she received a call from Nelson's assistant.

"Ms. Esposito, I'm calling to inform you that Colco has decided not to renew your contract in light of our prospective outlook," her voice droned.

"You're not renewing? And this is your excuse? I'll have you know that this is against the law. It's discrimination. I won't stand for it."

The assistant terminated the call, leaving Carmen hurt and confused. The friendly relationship that she and her onetime clients had established had been destroyed in one afternoon. Her threats were empty. In her heart, she understood they no longer liked her much.

Carmen yielded to forgiveness and did not allow the loss to upset her further. By forgiving the shortsightedness of her former clients, she would at least be free from their negativity.

Wisdom to Take Away

- It is impossible to go through the process of building a business without someone doing something that harms you. Whether the person acts intentionally or not, the result to you is the same. You will feel hurt and will find it easy to hold a grudge or to seek revenge for the damage done to you and your company.
- Hate, retribution, and vengeance are enormous drains on human energy, creativity, and enlightenment.

These emotions, though understandable, will sap your energy and remove the fun from the entrepreneurial process.

- The principle of forgiveness commands that when you are wronged by people, you immediately seek to forgive them, perhaps by confronting them and sharing your forgiveness. Even after you forgive them, never turn your back on them again, and always watch them with a wary eye. But by forgiving them, you remove the burden from your shoulders and place it where it belongs—on theirs.

WEEK

44

The Listen to Your Inner Voice Principle

The Search Party

Ashana enjoyed the early years of her career as a systems engineer for IBM. She had felt on top of the world when she received a job offer from Big Blue after graduating near the top of her class from the University of Colorado. She was proud of her success, and she knew her Mama's prayers and hard work had allowed her to complete the program in four years, when most of her peers had taken five.

Ashana accepted the IBM job and Ashana relocated to Tampa, Florida. The move proved to be excellent for her personally and professionally. Her job responsibilities quickly grew, and it soon became clear that Ashana was good for IBM and that IBM was good for her. She excelled in computer design and development and was highly valued for her engineering, scientific, and manufacturing knowledge. It seemed that overnight she became an engineering and marketing sensation, and she was instrumental in building her marketing territory into one of the fastest growing in the company.

In the beginning of her third year, the job began to lose its appeal. In spite of her stellar success, Ashana's heart wasn't in her work. No matter how much IBM valued her or how much she was compensated, she could no longer ignore her secret desire to become an entrepreneur. After consulting with former classmates and business advisors, she left IBM to start up her own telecommunications consulting firm, TCG.

Within weeks, Ashana negotiated her first contract. She knew it was important to bring business in quickly. She worked hard to impress her sole client, and the project went well. But while Ashana devoted all her attention to it, she ignored the need to continue marketing to gain new clients. As a result, once her first contract was completed, Ashana had no business.

Ashana panicked and embarked on a mad search for "quick hits." She started attending every minority and female entrepreneur business conference in her region; searched the Internet and the local newspapers for notices of upcoming contract opportunities; and contacted everyone in her database for piecework. Disappointing days flowed into sleepless nights, which led to worry-filled weeks that dragged into depressing months. "I can't believe this is happening to me!" she thought. "Every strategy I've tried has failed. Maybe I'm just not cut out for this. Maybe I should go back to IBM."

Ashana sat at her oversized desk staring at her old IBM awards decorating the walls, wondering if the company would rehire her. The phone rang and startled her back to reality. She was tempted to let the answering machine take the call, but finally assumed her successful businesswoman's voice and lifted the receiver.

"Hello, you've reached the offices of TCG. Can I help you?"

"Hey! This is Cheryl," chirped the voice on the other end. "I hadn't heard from you and was checking to see if you're going to the retreat this weekend. It's gonna be fun."

"Honey, I can't go anywhere," Ashana moaned. "I've got to work on these proposals or I won't be able to eat next month."

"Girl, one weekend away from the office is not going to make or break you. Besides, you've been stuck in that office by yourself for too long."

"You're right about that," Ashana agreed, "but if I don't get some business in here soon I'm going to have to move in with you."

Cheryl laughed. "If you're talking about moving into my tiny apartment, I know you're working too hard. You need to get away. I'll pick you up at 3:00 tomorrow."

The mountains and lake at the retreat were beautiful. It was early fall, and although the leaves had not begun to change colors yet, the smell of autumn was very much in the air. Ashana realized it had been too long since she had been away from the city; the warm sun on her face felt good. She and Cheryl leisurely walked around the big lake, watching adults and children playing in the paddleboats and canoeing. As Cheryl chatted about the new man in her life, a crowd gathering by the lakeshore caught Ashana's attention. A canoe had tipped over spilling a family into the lake. The parents were frantically trying to rescue their three young children.

A few men standing at the shore also saw what was happening and jumped into the lake to help. Within moments two children stood dripping on the bank pulling off their life jackets. Their soaked parents were wrapping their baby brother in a dry jacket. One of the rescuers, Trent, was shivering from both the cold and the excitement and retrieved his dry jacket. As he put it on, he reached into the pocket for his eyeglasses; they weren't there. Trent suddenly realized he hadn't taken them off before plunging into the water. His glasses were undoubtedly somewhere at the bottom of the lake.

By lunchtime, word had spread about the hero who had lost his glasses. Three participants in the retreat, including Ashana, decided they would brave the lake's cold water and try to find the glasses.

As the three swimmers waded into the cold water, a large crowd gathered on the shore. Ashana was the first to plunge into the dark, cold depths of the lake. She propelled herself toward the bottom through the murky water. She tried to open her eyes, but the water was like pea soup. To make matters worse, the lake bottom was soft and slippery.

After two hours in the cold water, the divers began to give up hope. One, his skin shriveled from the cold water and his eyes burning from the algae, said he needed a break and went ashore. Ashana heard him whisper to the other, "There's no way we'll ever find Trent's glasses. Let's just take up a collection and help the brother buy some new ones." Soon the other diver followed suit, leaving Ashana alone in the water.

Trent beckoned to Ashana to give up the search. As she started for the shore, Ashana uttered a short prayer. "Lord, please help me find Trent's glasses." Something inside her whispered, "You can find those glasses. Keep trying and don't give up." Making her way toward the shore, Ashana continued diving to the bottom of the lake, but she tried a different tactic. Instead of trying to see her way in the watery depths, she began feeling her way by moving her hands in a circular motion in an attempt to cover as much area as possible. It didn't work.

Ashana tried one last time. She dived to the bottom of the lake, spread out her arms, and laid flat. Just as before, she heard a quiet voice that instructed her to dig down into the muddy lake floor. Without questioning, Ashana started digging and quickly pulled up a handful of mud, gravel— and a pair of wire-rimmed glasses.

Ashana was quiet as she and Cheryl drove back to the city. Ashana replayed in her mind the amazing events of the weekend. Cheryl understood and was comfortable with the silence. Exhausted from the swim and the excitement, Ashana drifted off to sleep while Cheryl safely navigated through the mountains.

Early Monday morning Ashana arrived in her office to pick up on her efforts to secure new business. She felt renewed, invigorated—and invulnerable. As she stared at the large pile of requests for proposals that had buried her desk, she smiled and chuckled to herself. "Hey, if God allowed me to find my way to a pair of glasses at the bottom of a large lake, He certainly will lead me to find my way to get business. All I have to do is to keep doing my part and He is certain to do his."

Wisdom to Take Away

- The demands of running a business require you as an entrepreneur to use all of your senses to lead you to the right decision. Your inner voice or intuition is probably your most trusted companion. The more you listen to your inner voice, the more you will learn to trust it. A Chinese philosopher once said: "There is no need to go outside for better seeing nor to peer from a window. Rather remain at the center of your being."

- At times the environment may be so murky that it's difficult to see what lies before you. While you use your sense of touch to discern the warmth of a handshake of a potential partner, or your sense of hearing to listen to the real message behind a customer's phone call, your inner voice is usually correct. Learn to listen for and listen to it. When you listen to that small voice from deep within and engage all of your senses, you can find success even when it is not at first apparent.

45

The Do What You Fear Principle

The Chain-Link Fence

My childhood friend Carl Jr. and I had a dangerous game we often played. In the housing projects where we lived, people enclosed their yards with steel chain-link fences. The fences varied in height. Some were two to three feet high, others much taller. They were intended to keep out burglars, stray dogs, and hardheaded little boys like Carl Jr. and me.

The neighbors didn't know that these fences never intimidated us. In fact, to us, they were an invitation. We would carefully walk along the top of the fence railing as part of a do-or-die test to see who could walk farther without losing balance and falling to the ground.

Failure to remain atop the rail could be painful, especially for prepubescent boys. And there was an element of danger if an unfriendly dog resided in the adjacent yard. Mrs. Hicks, my next-door neighbor, had a big, dirty German shepherd named Rex. Rex was the ugliest, meanest dog in the neighborhood—a true junkyard dog by anyone's standards. Mrs. Hicks's son, Phillip, had trained the dog to be vicious and to attack anyone who stepped into their back-yard. All of us boys knew that getting caught in Mrs. Hicks's yard was the kiss of death.

One afternoon, looking to make our game more challenging, Carl Jr. and I decided to test our nerves and balancing skills on Mrs. Hicks's fence. Carl Jr. went first. He walked the entire length of the fence without falling, although Rex followed him barking ferociously and jumping wildly trying to get at Carl's pant legs. Carl reached the last post, jumped to safety, and challenged me. "Okay, now you do it!'

Nervously I mounted the rail and took two steps before I saw Rex bound in my direction. I prided myself on being a good athlete and had often bragged that I could beat Carl Jr. in any sport. I struggled to keep my balance on the fence. Rex's bark got louder.

As I looked down to see how close Rex was, the unthinkable happened. I lost my balance and landed in Mrs. Hicks's yard, about five feet from Rex. My fall must have startled him, because he froze for a moment before starting toward me. My athletic ability paid off—I was on my feet and tearing across the yard in a split second. Before Rex could reach me, I vaulted over the fence, and although I cut my hand in the process, I felt lucky to have escaped Rex. Panting to catch my breath, I spotted Carl Jr. standing in my backyard with his mouth hanging open.

By now my hand had started to burn, and I knew something else would burn when I got home and Momma saw the close to nasty tear in my school pants.

"How come you can always walk this fence without falling even when Rex is trying to get you?" I asked.

"It's easy," Carl said. "First of all, whenever I'm on the fence, I never think about Rex. Yeah, I hear him barking, but when I'm in motion I sort of tune him out. Besides, I'm not worried about his bite anyway. I figure even if Rex does bite me, his bite won't kill me. The next thing is, I don't worry about how high the fence is. It doesn't matter if the fence is two feet or twenty-two feet off the ground—I just don't think about it. I just keep my eye on the last post of the fence. That last post is where I want to get to, so I focus on it.

"Besides, I know I can make it to the end of the fence without falling because I've already done it. The more I do it, the easier it becomes and the less I fear it."

Wisdom to Take Away

- Successful entrepreneurs condition themselves to do what they fear because they know the more they accomplish a particular task, the less they fear it.
- Success means that you focus on the objective and not on the surrounding "noise." Noise is anything that acts to deter you or causes you to magnify the inherent risks and costs of failure.
- Faith overcomes fear, and the defeat of fear breeds success. Success leads to ultimate power over the noise.

PART FOUR

The Principles of Self-Actualization

WEEK
46

The Game Within
the Game Principle

The Chess Game

Chess had been a favorite game of Dana Coleman's since her childhood. She and her uncles spent countless hours playing, plotting, and strategizing their next fatal move. She loved the inner workings of the game. She called it "the game within the game." She meant that the relationship established by two opposing forces can have quirky beginnings and endings.

Given her lifelong love of strategy and tactical maneuvers, it was no wonder she became a lawyer. One of her chess-playing uncles, Lance, was already a well-respected lawyer and a partner in his practice by the time she was in grade school.

Dana graduated at the top of her law class and passed the bar exam on the first try. She practiced civil law for her uncle's firm, Brackman and Associates, preferring to stay away from the types of cases she had seen as a clerk in the district attorney's office. She had a hectic trial schedule, but on weekends she also maintained a small private practice that yielded not only profit but also a true sense of purpose.

Coleman Legal Consultation provided legal advice and paralegal services to the community and to people who couldn't afford a lawyer.

In her first year of this part-time practice, Dana realized her love of chess would come in handy.

Harvey Jinson was an ex-con with a history that could have been the script for a Fox Channel movie of the week. He had started burglarizing at age ten, was arrested for armed robbery at twelve, and was convicted of manslaughter at fifteen. He appeared in her office one afternoon with lowered head and sad eyes, looking for advice.

"I don't want to lie to you, ma'am. They're right about my past. I've done a lot of things, but what they're accusing me of, I didn't do. I served my time, five years, and I don't want to go back. Never."

His words tugged at her. She believed him and decided to help.

She did some digging and found—to her dismay—he was being harassed by a senior partner at Brackman and Associates. Robert Brackman, Jr., the son of the founder, was threatening to fine and prosecute Harvey for destruction of property. Harvey was a night janitor, one of the few given access to the executive-level suite. Certain files were missing and later mysteriously found in the basement near Harvey's janitorial station.

Dana felt uncomfortable. If she continued to advise Harvey, it could be viewed as a conflict of interest within her firm. If she didn't, her conscience would bother her to no end. She decided to take a different tack and put this problem to rest immediately.

Dana called Harvey back to her office to clarify the details. She then called the firm. "Hi, this Dana Coleman. Is Rob Brackman available?" As she made the call, Harvey fidgeted nervously.

Dana held back a laugh. "Rob, this is Dana. I just received word that a Mr. Harvey Jinson is being blamed for destroying files. I hope you'll reconsider—we both know what a terrible time the firm had last year when the same situation occurred and it turned out to be an internal error. Just wanted to drop you that little bug. Bye."

Dana released her laugh. "Not to worry, Mr. Jinson. I don't think anyone is going to be fired."

"Why is that?" His face registered both confusion and joy.

"I play the game, sir. So does Rob Brackman. The trick is to find a tactical way to take the upper hand. Brackman probably blamed you because he didn't have a better excuse at the time. He was looking for a convenient scapegoat. The bottom line is he can't fire you for those reasons and he knows it, but he knew that you didn't know it."

"So I'm the scapegoat, eh?" Jinson's face sank.

"Not anymore. Now they know that I am watching them. Expect a call."

"I still don't quite understand it all."

"Do you play chess?"

Dana's question summed up the situation, and he smiled at her with understanding.

Dana had found a way out of the predicament for Harvey and for herself by using her childhood love of chess to play "the game within the game."

Wisdom to Take Away

- Success in business is often compared to sports because both are primarily male dominated. The team that has scored the most points at the end of the allotted time is declared the winner. However, there is "the game within the game." Its plays are subtle—not as obvious as the big game. Whatever the situation, there are always subplots within the game that astute players must recognize and use to their advantage in order to win.

- Entrepreneurs must perfect their level of understanding of the game within the game. Failure to understand these dynamics will result in wasted resources and missed opportunities.

WEEK

47

The Three Spiritual Retreats Principle

The Dull Boy

"That's it! I'm officially going nuts!" Greg Hall bellowed from his office. His assistant, Dario Jimenez, slipped into the inner office and closed the door softly. Greg was at his wit's end again. His business, Graphix, Inc., was causing him more stress than enjoyment.

Dario was his only full-time employee—he wanted to keep his operation small. Though Greg was criticized by some colleagues who had larger staffs, many of them had barely survived the winter downtime due to bloated overhead and expenses.

"Listen, Greg," Dario began, "maybe you should take a few days off. I can manage the accounts, and Luisa and Chuck will be in again for a few hours this week."

Greg had not taken a vacation since he started Graphix nearly two years ago. He invested all his energy and resources in making it a success. Only months into opening he landed major accounts with two local businesses, an electronics supply store and an exclusive boutique. These and several other customers kept the group very busy.

"Vacation? You know me better than that, Dar. Maybe I'll just leave early on Friday. How about seven?"

Dario knew Greg was serious. For Greg, leaving at seven o'clock was early. "People think you're crazy, Greg. You need to enjoy what you've earned. If I had my own business running smoothly, I'd finally be able to relax."

Greg chuckled. "Dar, you see me sweating it out every day here. You must know how hard it is."

"But it couldn't be easier. My cousin runs his own chain of video stores. He keeps a small staff so he can basically manage them without interference. He hires a manager and bang!—just like that he has time to enjoy his money."

Greg didn't want to argue with Dario about the rigors of opening a business or the inconsistency of this analogy. "I'm sure your cousin has a better setup than I do. I can't go anywhere. Not now."

"Listen, Greg. You aren't married or anything. You've got the money. Even if you didn't, I'd tell you the same thing. All work and no play makes Jack dot, dot, dot."

Greg smiled. He knew Dario was sincere and was probably right. In the past month, Greg had slept at home only eight nights; the others he stayed at the office. When he played his phone messages, he'd hear at least a dozen from his mother reminding him to eat, sleep, and take care of himself.

"You may be on to something, Dar. I know I need to rest, but I don't know how. All I've thought about in so long is this business—these walls, my PC, my overhead." Greg was obsessing. "I have to stay, Dar. How could I leave?"

"You have to. I don't want to pull any more punches, Greg. The fact is you're burned out. You're out of juice. This place will be fine for a while. Mostly, we're maintaining our current accounts. We need you to be up to your best. Now stop making me into a mother hen and get out of here."

Dario grabbed Greg's jacket from the coatrack. He snatched his boss's briefcase and dumped several folders from it. Then he hoisted Greg to his feet and escorted him out of the office and into the hallway of the building. Greg didn't have the strength to resist.

"I'm doing this for your own good, Greg. Take a break!" The door slammed. Greg had been politely thrown out of his own office. He wanted to laugh, but the silence in the hallway quieted him. He really did need a vacation.

After a week in Maui, Greg phoned into the office to find that the world had not ended. Armageddon did not come. It felt great to spend a little time and money just on himself. So he stayed away a second week, this time in Bali. Greg found that getting away allowed him to recharge and regain perspective.

Wisdom to Take Away

- The worst thing that can happen to entrepreneurs is to get burned out. The daily rigors of starting, growing, and maintaining a business are extremely taxing on physical, mental, and spiritual resources.
- Since your spiritual self gives you the fuel of life and ambition, it is critical that you maintain and strengthen that part of you. This strengthening can be achieved by making sure that you schedule a few spiritual retreats each year.
- Spiritual retreats will be different for different people. Some retreats are available through church, temple, or synagogue. Even a week alone with your spouse in the mountains or at the beach could mean a great deal.

WEEK

48

The Getting in Contact with How You Learn Principle

Securing the Future

Education specialists spend time and money to study the cognitive process. How people learn can be instrumental in their pursuit of happiness. Researchers have discovered a threefold process containing visual, audio, and kinesthetic learning:

Visual learning works best for those people who need to be "in the moment" to learn new things. They usually rely on visually organizing notes and ideas in order to bolster understanding.

Audio learning works best for those whose listening skills are honed. They usually rely on spoken words or tapes to enhance the learning process.

Kinesthetic learning works best for those who need a hands-on approach. They rely on doing. Also, kinesthetic learners tend to have a visual element to their learning. They may rely on the act of taking notes.

Combination learning is just that. It involves using two or more of the above processes.

Specialists have found that learning is a process that requires an open mind. Any resistance is usually a blockage to the process.

Wisdom to Take Away

- Every entrepreneur learns differently. For some, learning requires being in a classroom eight hours a day with an instructor. They require a formal curriculum in a structured environment. Others learn better by using computer-based training programs and studying on their own when it is convenient. Web-based training systems are projected to experience exponential growth in the new millennium. Some entrepreneurs are already using these advanced technologies to keep up with their field.
- Don't make the mistake of assuming that because one learning technique works for someone else that it will automatically work for you.
- Remember that learning is a lifelong process. Plan on learning new and exciting things as long as you live.

49

The Principle of
the Flying Geese

The V Formation

Edwin made every attempt to understand what Dr. Kiyoshi Yeh, distinguished professor of mechanical engineering and applied mechanics, was saying. Dr. Yeh, world-renowned for his groundbreaking research on fluid and thermal dynamics, was using the analogy of flying geese as an introduction to his course on airplane design.

Edwin felt honored to be in Dr. Yeh's class but was frustrated because Dr. Yeh spoke with a strong Japanese accent that made it difficult for the students to follow his lectures. It was especially hard for Edwin, who was raised in southeast Washington, D.C., and was unaccustomed to heavily accented English.

Despite the communication challenges between Dr. Yeh and his students, Edwin became intrigued with the analogy of the flying geese and the design of airplanes and their wing structure. He listened intently—and learned. He earned his bachelor's degree in mechanical engineering and applied mechanics and started his own aerospace engineering consulting firm.

Many years later, Edwin could still recall Dr. Yeh's lecture, and he used it as an analogy to explain the challenges and opportunities facing minority and female entrepreneurs.

"Dr. Yeh taught that there are scientific reasons why geese fly in a V formation. Scientists have discovered that as each bird flaps its wings, it creates what are called vortices at the tips of their wings. These vortices are small masses of air that move in a circular motion (like a whirlpool) and form a cavity or vacuum in the middle of the circulating air pockets, creating an uplift. Thus, each bird creates an uplift for the bird immediately behind it, which means the bird behind has to work a little less than the bird in front in order to achieve the same level of velocity and lift. There is also a compounding benefit achieved that benefits the entire flock. The vorticity created by all of the flapping birds allows the birds near the end of the formation to fly with the flock while exerting little or no effort. The overall benefit is that the flock is able to increase its flying range by 75 percent compared to the range each bird could fly on its own."

Edwin continued his explanation. "Another point that Dr. Yeh made was that the geese take turns leading the formation. When the lead goose tires, he rotates to the rear of the formation and another goose takes the lead. To encourage one another, the geese behind the lead will occasionally honk as a motivational call to the flock to encourage the birds to keep up their pace and not to grow weary. But what I found most amazing about the story of the geese is that when a goose is wounded by gunshot or gets sick and has to leave the flock to rest somewhere, two geese fall out of formation and stay with the fallen goose until it either heals or dies. The separated geese then take off in their own miniature V formation and fly to catch up with the group.

"I have never forgotten the power of Dr. Yeh's illustration. I have lived by the teachings of this wildlife analogy, and it has served me and my entrepreneurial peers very well over the years."

Wisdom to Take Away

- The flight of an entrepreneur, if taken alone, can be a lonely and difficult journey. Although many attempt it, taking this journey alone is neither necessary nor prudent.
- Whatever direction you as an entrepreneur desire to take, remember that there are people who have either already been where you're trying to go or who are in the process of taking the same journey. Seek out those who are heading in the same direction and figure out together how you can all get to your destination more quickly and with less wear and tear.
- Once you're confident that you've built a support group that shares your vision of the ultimate destination, encourage members to step up at the right time and take the lead for the group. Each situation that the group finds itself in may require a different set of skills in order to master the situation. As the group members get to know one another, they will understand who has strengths in which areas and thus know who should lead at any given time. For example, an entrepreneur who has strengths in the financial industry maybe should lead when there are financial or accounting issues confronting the group. If another member has an operations-type background, that person could lead in directing the group on how to attain operational efficiencies during times of slow business growth.
- Another important lesson to learn from the geese is that like-minded entrepreneurs must learn to stand by one another during each person's "dry season." A dry season signifies those periods of our business journey

when things don't go our way—when everything
seems to go wrong and nothing we try seems to work.
Our need for support and encouragement is greatest
during these times. It is comforting to know that there
are other people out there who will be with us no
matter what comes our way. And remember that it is
just a matter of time before you'll be going through
your own dry season.

- Last, maybe the most important lesson from the principle of the flying geese is that group members should
learn to encourage one another and share each others'
burdens.

50

The Wealth by Permission Principle

The Lottery

Latisha won the lottery. She had played for years with little success, but now she had won over five million dollars.

Latisha's sister Gabrielle broke the good news to family and friends despite Latisha's reservations about making the news public. She wanted her close family members to know but was concerned that so many others would expect her to share the winnings.

She knew she needed to invest in college funds for her two small children, Bria and Kobe, to make sure their future was set. Her dilemma was what to do with the money in the ten years before Bria would be a freshman.

She was generous with her family and her two closest friends but didn't buy anything extravagant for herself. She put the kids in private school but drove her nine-year-old Dodge to drop them off each morning. Latisha's frugality was met with constant criticism from her family. Her mother forced her to buy new clothes; without the coercion, Latisha would have continued wearing her three-year-old winter coat.

She kept her job until her brother sold her half of his Clemmons Enterprises, which was diversified ownership of a yogurt shop, a strip mall, and an ATM manufacturer. At first the business struggled, but within six months its profit margin increased fivefold. Latisha once again was financially bolstered. She gave to family and friends again, this time offering job opportunities as well. Bria and Kobe had their best Christmas to date, but Latisha still refused to purchase more than the necessities for herself.

"You've got some kind of Midas touch, girl," her sister Shelly remarked over lunch one afternoon.

"I don't care about having a golden touch. I just want my kids to have a better chance at life than we did." Latisha was the oldest of four. She knew very well how her parents had struggled to keep things together.

"But they already have a much better chance. You're richer than any of us—not that you'd know it by the way you look." Shelly snickered.

"I don't need to be insulted." Latisha feigned anger. She knew her sister had the best of intentions.

"All I'm saying is that you've finally reached a place in your life when you don't have to struggle anymore. You should enjoy it."

"What if I start having all the fun you and everyone else keep talking about and I lose everything? What then?" Latisha was certain Shelly had no answer.

"You could lose it by making a mistake on your taxes. Anything could happen. Still, you have to allow yourself to experience the joy now. You have it now. You saw Mom and Dad when they were struggling. Do you think that if they had become financially blessed, they wouldn't have celebrated it by improving their quality of life?"

Shelly made sense. She had a knack for making sense out of great confusion. The idea had been proposed so many times, but when Shelly brought their parents into it, it began to become clear. Latisha had been neglecting herself.

"So you think I should start spending on myself just like that?"

"Stop asking me. It's your money. It's your blessing. Don't neglect it. You don't need me to say it's okay as long as you can believe it for yourself."

Latisha began to realize the freedom her wealth gave her. She had simply chosen to live like a prisoner. She had been waiting for permission to do what didn't require permission.

Wisdom to Take Away

- Minority entrepreneurs have often been stymied in the creation of wealth not only by the racist and sexist policies and institutions that tend to resist this wealth creation but also by the fact that some feel the need for permission from some unknown force to achieve any level of wealth.
- The only permission you need is from within. Listen for it.

WEEK
51

The Principle of Partnering with God

Mumbles

The childhood part of my life wasn't very pretty.
You see I was born and raised in the slums of the City.
It was a one room shack and I slept with 10 other children beside me.
We hardly had enough room and food to eat.
It was hard times; I needed something to ease my troubled mind.
My father didn't know the meaning of work.
He disrespected Momma and treated us like dirt.
I left home seeking a job that I never did find.
Depressed and downhearted I took to cloud nine.
I'm doing fine, on Cloud Nine!
  "Runaway Child," The Temptations, Motown Records

This popular song by The Temptations illustrated the experiences of many young black men in America during the 1960s and 1970s. It was especially appropriate for a troubled young man nicknamed Mumbles.

The guys in the projects called him Mumbles because, like the despicable character in the Dick Tracy comics, this young man suffered from a severe speech impediment. He couldn't say his own name without stuttering. No matter how hard he tried to carry on a conversation with his peers, the words became garbled in his throat and emerged from his mouth in a low, deep mumble. His speech problem worsened when he started school because his teachers forced him to attend speech class in order to help him. For him, however, the classes were punishment, because class-mates often ridiculed him.

The speech classes were helpful, but Mumbles's teachers began to suspect that maybe the reason he stuttered so bad-ly stemmed from his dysfunctional family environment. Raised in the gritty, drug-infested, violent projects of South Baltimore, Mumbles shared living quarters not only with five brothers but also a colony of nasty, filthy rats, a legion of roaches, and a troubled father who sometimes drank too much and physically abused his mother. When Mumbles's parents ran out of money and were unable to pay the water and heating bills, the children went without bathing for days and wore their coats in the house to keep warm. They had to borrow water from the neighbors and heated it on a gas stove to use for cooking and washing. At night, the boys huddled two or three to a bed bundled in their coats.

Over time, the stress of physical harm from her husband and of having three of her boys serving tours in Vietnam plunged Mumbles's mother into despair. To relieve her pain, she reluctantly turned to alcohol as an escape. Alco-hol soon gained the upper hand, and one day she woke up and realized she was an alcoholic. Mumbles later found out that his favorite uncle, Bill, his mother's oldest brother, was also an alcoholic who struggled with the disease and with depression for years.

Although all three of Mumbles's brothers returned from Vietnam, the war took its toll on them. About the same time, Mumbles began spending more time living on the streets. Although he was a good student academically during the day, at night he hung out with drug addicts, stick-up artists, alcoholics, gang-bangers, purse snatchers, glue sniffers, and marijuana smokers. Very few in Mumbles's gang ever made it beyond high school. Many of them ended up either in prison, murdered, or mentally and emotionally destroyed by years of alcohol and drug abuse. Mumbles's life and future prospects were spiraling progressively downward.

One Saturday night, Mumbles attended a party across town with friends, even though his mother had refused to give her permission. He sneaked out the back door after she passed out over her whiskey bottle. That night Mumbles and three companions were brutally attacked by a mob of youths from a hostile neighborhood across town. Although guns were pulled, knives were drawn, and baseball bats collided, Mumbles and his companions survived the ordeal with their lives changed but intact.

Feeling that God had clearly intervened to spare his life, Mumbles gratefully stumbled homeward in the early morning darkness. With his pants wet with urine and his shirt soaked with perspiration and the warm blood from freshly opened cuts, Mumbles hurried through the back door and toward the steps leading to his bedroom. He prayed that his mother was still passed out.

As he passed the kitchen, he saw his mother sitting at the kitchen table having a conversation with someone. She was still drinking and was quite intoxicated but was talking to an unseen person. Mumbles knew no one else was in the house. Puzzled, he moved closer to the kitchen door so that he could hear and see better.

His mother was holding herself, her arms across her chest, and rocking back and forth in her chair uncontrollably. "Please, Lord, please save me and my children. Please,

Lord, please save us. Lord, I don't want to live like this, and my children deserve better. Please save us!"

His mother was talking to God. Mumbles entered the kitchen, touched his mother's shoulders, and mother and son dropped to their knees and began to pray.

After that night Mumbles's life changed dramatically. Although he still loved his friends in the neighborhood, he slowly withdrew from their company, choosing instead to take school more seriously. He was an excellent student and won a scholarship to an Ivy League university. He met and married a beautiful young woman, and they had five children together. He later attended another Ivy League university for graduate studies before launching a number of businesses, and in the process he became a popular motivational speaker. Obviously, Mumbles overcame his stuttering problem.

Mumbles's mother began attending Alcoholics Anonymous (AA) meetings and soon thereafter stopped drinking. She later enrolled in the local university and earned her bachelor's degree in education, a master's in child psychology, and credits toward her Ph.D. She retired from the local school system after twenty-five years of teaching and influencing the lives of hundreds of severely underprivileged children.

Bill joined his sister at AA meetings, and he too stopped drinking. He resumed his career as a teacher in the county school system and became an instrumental player in the fight for civil rights and integration around the country. Mumbles's brother and his childhood friend Kenny turned away from drugs and alcohol and turned instead to God. Both men became ministers and preached the word of God with great passion and conviction.

Mumbles's experience is an example of the amazing things we can do when we partner with God instead of fighting him.

Wisdom to Take Away

- We all want the world to recognize us and value us for who we are and for what we can contribute to society. Unfortunately, the world defines greatness in a misleading and confusing manner. To some, greatness is defined in terms of who has the most material assets (money, land, automobiles, real estate). Others define greatness by how much power a person possesses or how well known a person is. All of these things—money, power, prestige—are fine if viewed with the proper perspective.

- To achieve true greatness in business or in our personal lives, however, we must pay attention to our spiritual side. The power of God (you can define God as you see fit) allows a weak, frightened, broken, fragile, underconfident, and imperfect person to go on to accomplish amazing feats.

- The secret to tapping into spiritual power is first to recognize that you're incomplete, inadequate, and in need of help. Mumbles was afraid and looking for answers. He stuttered and was bowlegged. He was confused and had lost all hope. His partnership with God changed all of that.

The Applause for
Doing a Good Job Principle

The Celebration

The office celebration lasted into the evening hours. Zander Jefferson and Sheila Williams hosted a jamboree for their staff of eleven and a few supportive friends in honor of their three-year anniversary. Buyitcheap.com was a smash success. The minority-owned and -operated e-commerce site was awash in business. Most Web sites employed fewer staff, but Zander and Sheila felt the extra help was money well spent. They never quibbled over salaries of employees, especially since most were contractual or part-time. Everyone genuinely liked one another. In fact, the surprise of the first year was when Margaret, the shy receptionist, married one of the site designers. The anniversary was a celebration of so many triumphs. It was a giant thank-you to all.

The dancing commenced. Peter, the accountant, was cutting his step with Vesta, the saucy sales consultant whose insight saved the site more than once. Zander loved sharing time with his staff. They were true people. Sheila found herself raucously laughing at the musings of Billy, the office assistant, whose humor enlivened dull days.

By nine o'clock, most people had departed, leaving Zander, Sheila, Billy, and Vesta. As they cleaned up the party litter, they reviewed the wild events of what was supposed to have been a simple celebration.

"I couldn't believe Irma and Margaret singing like that. And we didn't have any liquor at the party," Billy remarked holding back a laugh.

"When people feel they've done a good job, they need to release it. Let's just be thankful it ended with two songs. I've seen Margaret do a miniconcert more than once," chimed Zander.

Sheila and Vesta began the final sweeping. "I can't tell you how glad I am that tomorrow is Saturday." Sheila beamed. She would be spending time with her kids and husband. "Tomorrow," she sighed, "tomorrow I get to pretend that I don't work anywhere, because we made it through another year and that means I can play, for a minute. I'll just hang out with my boys. Wait a minute! Did I say that?"

"You know you love it, girl. You and Larry have a great time with the kids every weekend," Zander observed.

"We're going to some amusement park tomorrow. The boys will run wild. We'll chase them. You're right. I love it! In fact, I think this is where I jump off this train. Good night, all." With that, she snatched up her belongings and swished out the door.

"What are you doing tomorrow, V?" Billy wondered.

"I'm taking an African dance class. I owe it to myself. I haven't done it in a while, but it should be fun." She trailed off into a monologue about dance history as she gathered the remaining party plates.

"What about you, Zan?" Vesta inquired.

But Zander couldn't hear her. He was already elsewhere in his mind. He knew that three years as a competitive site was quite an accomplishment. Now he wanted to be in lush green landscapes melded together in a thick carpet of color, where the air was rarefied and the water was pure: his favorite climb, Mt. Henrick near his mother's home. He loved to climb it when he was celebrating an achievement.

"Zan?" Billy assisted Vesta's inquiry.

Zander needed to be there. He grabbed his coat and keys and headed out the door, calling his answer over his shoulder. "My mountain."

He drove all night to get to his mountain, but this was his personal celebration.

Wisdom to Take Away

- The rewards for doing a good job should be whatever you want them to be. You could take a trip or invest in the arts. Whatever engages your spirit should be your applause for doing a good job. While you're at it, enjoy the standing ovation.

Epilogue

I have a confession to make. If you haven't figured it out yet, "Mumbles," the young man in the story, is none other than myself, Robert L. Wallace. I'm sure that my experiences growing up in the low-income housing projects of the city are not unique. I would bet that some of you have your own Mumbles story that you could share. Maybe you have a Mumbles in your family or you personally know someone who displayed the reckless attributes that I displayed as a young black man growing up in south Baltimore.

As I look back on my experiences as Mumbles, surviving in the "hood," it quickly dawns on me that one of the reasons that I and others were able to survive and learn from that childhood experience was the fact that I was taught, and quickly learned, what the unwritten rules of the street were—the principles of success, if you will.

Understanding and mastering the principles of success also served me well when I attended the University of Pennsylvania and the Tuck School of Business at Dartmouth College. At the time, the concept of an Ivy League University was quite foreign to me. The truth be told, I thought that Ivy League was the name of some cologne that men wore. Nevertheless, I began my career at Pennsylvania operating under the mistaken belief that since I was intelligent, academically successful, and highly motivated, that I could be successful at this university, all by myself, and didn't need anyone's help. I was very wrong.

It wasn't until I learned about the principle of collaboration, that I began making even more impressive academic strides. Likewise at Dartmouth, it wasn't until I mastered the principle of focused effort that I began to enjoy the experience of business school and exceed the goals that I had established for myself.

Like my experiences as a young boy and then as a student, I have also learned, as an entrepreneur, that in this exciting world of business, there are principles and "rules of engagement" that we need to understand in order to be successful.

As I began the research for my first book *Black Wealth through Black Entrepreneurship* and my followup second book, *Black Wealth: The Road to Small Business Success* I was blessed to have had the opportunity to converse with hundreds of minority and female entrepreneurs about the principles of entrepreneurial success from a minority and female perspective. I listened intently and learned.

The stories and principles that you have just read are the compilation of those intimate discussions with these special people. I hope that you have taken your time with each of these principles and allowed them to marinade in your mind and heart. Put them to use, refer to them frequently, and share them with others. But above all, take action and seek your own level of success, accomplishment, and happiness. *Soul Food* was written for just that purpose.

Index

About the Author

Robert L. Wallace is an author, entrepreneur, management consultant, and lecturer. He is founder and CEO of two companies—The BiTH Group, Inc. (www.Bithgroup.com) and EntreTeach.com (www.EntreTeach.com). The BiTH Group provides information-technology consulting services to government and commercial clients. EntreTeach. com provides Web-based training and business support services via the Internet for minority, female, and youth entrepreneurs as well as for corporate intrapreneurs. He is a highly sought after speaker and talk show host.

Robert earned his undergraduate degree in mechanical engineering and applied mechanics from the University of Pennsylvania and his MBA from the Tuck School of Business at Dartmouth College. He has more than twenty-four years of experience with such corporations as IBM, Procter & Gamble, Westinghouse, DuPont, and ECS Technologies. He has lectured at such universities as Dartmouth, University of Pennsylvania, University of Michigan, Howard University, Morgan University, and the University of Eastern Africa in Baraton, Kenya. He received a doctorate of Humane Letters from Sojourner-Douglass College.

Mr. Wallace serves on numerous corporate and civic boards, including those of Associated Black Charities, the Chapman Company, Gilman School, Maryland Works Inc., and the GE Center for Financial Learning (www.financial-learning.com). He is married to the former Carolyn A. Green and resides with his family in Ellicott City, Maryland.